The Touche Ross Tax Guide for the Family 1987/88

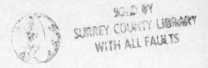

The Touche Ross Tax Guide for the Family 1987/88

BILL PACKER, MA, FCA

National Tax Technical Director
Touche Ross

and

COLIN SANDY, ATII

Tax Manager
Touche Ross

M
PAPERMAC

First published 1986 by
PAPERMAC
A division of Macmillan Publishers Limited
4 Little Essex Street London WC2R 3LF
and Basingstoke

Associated companies in Auckland, Delhi, Dublin, Gaborone, Hamburg, Harare, Hong Kong, Johannesburg, Kuala Lumpur, Lagos, Manzini, Melbourne, Mexico City, Nairobi, New York, Singapore and Tokyo

Second edition published 1987

British Library Cataloguing in Publication Data
Packer, Bill
    The Touche Ross tax guide for the family.——2nd ed.
    1. Taxation——Great Britain
    I. Title   II. Sandy, Colin
    336.2'00941   HJ2619

    ISBN 0-333-44961-4

Typeset by Wessex Typesetters
(Division of The Eastern Press Ltd),
Frome, Somerset
Printed by Richard Clay plc, Bungay, Suffolk

Contents

Preface to the 1987/88 Edition   xiii

1. THE SINGLE PERSON
    1.1   Principles of personal taxation   1
    1.2   Income tax   2
           1.2.1 Schedule A   3
           1.2.2 Schedule B   4
           1.2.3 Schedule C   4
           1.2.4 Schedule D   4
           1.2.5 Schedule E   12
           1.2.6 Schedule F   14
    1.3   Investment income   14
           1.3.1 Interest received   15
           1.3.2 Bank and building society
                  interest received   16
           1.3.3 Dividends received from UK
                  companies   17
           1.3.4 Dividends received from
                  overseas companies   18
    1.4   Deductions   19
           1.4.1 Personal allowances   19
           1.4.2 Interest paid   21

        1.4.3   Deeds of covenant   24
        1.4.4   Maintenance payments   25
    1.5   Capital gains tax   26
        1.5.1   Introduction   26
        1.5.2   Indexation allowance   27
        1.5.3   Annual exemption   28
        1.5.4   Losses   28
        1.5.5   Exempt assets   29
        1.5.6   Holdover relief   32
        1.5.7   Retirement relief   33
        1.5.8   Roll-over relief   35
    1.6   Inheritance tax   36
        1.6.1   Introduction   36
        1.6.2   Tax-free gifts   37
        1.6.3   Business reliefs   43
        1.6.4   Valuation of estate   45
        1.6.5   Settlements   46
        1.6.6   Paying the tax   49
    1.7   National insurance contributions   50

2. THE MARRIED MAN
    2.1   Introduction   52
    2.2   Year of marriage   54
    2.3   Separate taxation of wife's earnings   54
    2.4   Separate assessment   58
    2.5   Death   59
    2.6   Tax disadvantages and possible reforms   60
        2.6.1   Mortgage interest   60
        2.6.2   Capital gains tax   60
        2.6.3   Deeds of covenant   61
        2.6.4   Children   61

2.6.5 Business expansion scheme 62
2.6.6 Inheritance tax 62
2.6.7 Possible reforms 62

3. CHILDREN
3.1 Tax position as part of the family unit 65
3.2 Deeds of covenant 66
  3.2.1 Parents 66
  3.2.2 Grandparents and other relatives 68
3.3 Planning for school fees 70
  3.3.1 Introduction 70
  3.3.2 School fees composition scheme 71
  3.3.3 Educational trust 72
  3.3.4 Fixed interest scheme 72
  3.3.5 Scheme using a temporary annuity 73
  3.3.6 Life assurance based scheme 73
  3.3.7 Unit trust regular savings scheme 74
  3.3.8 Funding from other sources 74
3.4 Bare trustee settlements 75

4. PLANNING FOR RETIREMENT AND OLD AGE
4.1 Introduction 76
4.2 State benefits 76
4.3 Occupational pension schemes 78
  4.3.1 Introduction 78
  4.3.2 Definition of 'final salary' 81
  4.3.3 Guaranteed minimum pension 82
4.4 Pension rights when changing jobs 82
4.5 Additional voluntary contributions 87
4.6 Self-employed retirement annuities 89

4.7	Self-administered schemes	92
4.8	Loan back arrangements	94
4.9	Sick-pay and disability schemes	95
4.10	Death-in-service and accident policies	96
4.11	'Top-hat' schemes	97
4.12	Personal pension schemes	98
4.13	Purchased life annuities	101
4.14	Home income plans	102

5. **PROVISION FOR THE NEXT GENERATION**

5.1	Tax-efficient giving	104
5.2	Lifetime planning using settlements	104
5.2.1	The discretionary settlement	105
5.2.2	The accumulation and maintenance settlement	108
5.2.3	The interest in possession settlement	109
5.2.4	The personal settlement	110
5.3	Funding the ultimate inheritance tax liability	110
5.3.1	Joint life and survivor policies	111
5.3.2	Death-in-service benefits	112

6. **MAKING A WILL**

6.1	Consequences of not making a will	114
6.2	Variation of the terms of a will	115
6.3	Two-year discretionary will	118
6.4	Survivorship clause	119
6.5	*Commorientes*	120

7. RESIDENCE ABROAD
   7.1 Introduction ... 122
   7.2 Non-tax considerations ... 122
   7.3 Domicile and residence ... 124
       7.3.1 Domicile ... 124
       7.3.2 Residence and ordinary residence ... 125
       7.3.3 Husband and wife ... 126
       7.3.4 Available accommodation ... 127
       7.3.5 Procedure ... 127
   7.4 Employment earnings ... 128
   7.5 Tax on other income of non-residents ... 132
       7.5.1 UK source income ... 132
       7.5.2 Non UK source income ... 132
   7.6 Personal allowances for non-residents ... 133
   7.7 Double taxation relief ... 138
       7.7.1 Employment earnings ... 138
       7.7.2 Other income ... 139
       7.7.3 The UK's double tax treaties ... 140
   7.8 Unremittable overseas income ... 142

8. REDUNDANCY AND UNEMPLOYMENT
   8.1 Termination payments ... 143
       8.1.1 Introduction ... 143
       8.1.2 Capital or income? ... 145
       8.1.3 Exempt lump sums ... 146
       8.1.4 The charge to tax ... 147
       8.1.5 PAYE ... 150
   8.2 Redundancy payments ... 151
   8.3 Restrictive covenants ... 153
   8.4 Variation of service agreements ... 156
   8.5 'Golden hellos' and 'handcuffs' ... 157

8.5.1   'Hellos'   157
8.5.2   'Handcuffs'   158
8.6   The employer's position   160
8.7   Long-service awards   162
8.8   Unemployment benefit   163

9.   SEPARATION AND DIVORCE
9.1   Introduction   164
9.2   Income tax   165
         9.2.1   Personal allowances   165
         9.2.2   Additional personal allowance   166
         9.2.3   Mortgage interest relief   166
         9.2.4   Maintenance payments   168
         9.2.5   School fees   173
         9.2.6   Small maintenance payments   174
9.3   Capital gains tax   175
9.4   Inheritance tax   177
9.5   Stamp duty   178
9.6   Wills   178

10. TAX-EFFICIENT INVESTMENTS
10.1   Investment strategy   180
10.2   Sheltering income   181
10.3   Identifying situations where action
         may be necessary   183
10.4   Principal private residence   184
10.5   Charitable giving   185

APPENDIX A
   Income tax rates and allowances 1987/88   188
APPENDIX B
   Capital taxes 1987/88   190
APPENDIX C
   National insurance contributions 1987/88   191
APPENDIX D
   Cars and car petrol 1987/88   193

Preface to the 1987/88 Edition

While the family is for many people a very important part of their life, it is perhaps less often thought of in relation to tax. Yet taxation can form a major ingredient in the financial planning of a family's affairs, and the successful use of the taxation rules can make a substantial difference to a family's fortunes. In particular, tax planning for the family should not be thought of only as a prerogative of the wealthy; in its context it can be equally apt to those of modest means.

We have set out in this book to look at the various stages which the family passes through in its development. Of necessity we start with the single person, using this to describe in brief the basic principles which apply to the various forms of tax to which we may all be subject. We then move on to marriage, bringing up children, retirement and looking ahead to the next generation. We also look at the effect of going abroad.

For a number of people redundancy and the termination, expected or unexpected, of their employment produce challenges that have to be grappled with. For others there is the traumatic problem of the breakdown of their marriage and all that that entails. We look at the tax implications of these situations as they affect the individual and his family.

We have also given thought to the criteria which an

individual should apply to his investment policy in the best interests of himself and the family. While every person has his own views on how he should save or spend his money, we believe that there are certain basic principles which should always be borne in mind.

As always, the application of the ideas contained in this book to any particular set of circumstances does require care and consideration and a full understanding of the relevant facts. In looking at a specific situation relating to their affairs, readers should always seek competent professional advice.

The book is based on our understanding of UK tax law and practice as it applied at 31 July 1987, taking account of the changes introduced in the two 1987 Finance Acts. In general it does not deal with earlier provisions except where these may be helpful in appreciating the present position.

Income tax is a tax on individuals and, except in a few particular instances, does not recognize any difference between the sexes. For simplicity throughout the book we have referred to the masculine gender, but this should be read as including the feminine wherever appropriate.

We would like to record our especial thanks to Lorraine Donovan, who with much patience translated our often contradictory thoughts into a readable typescript.

London 1987

WRP
CTS

1 The Single Person

1.1 PRINCIPLES OF PERSONAL TAXATION

Although taxation in some form or another has been around for as long as there has been any form of civilized society, *income tax* was introduced into Britain only in 1799 to raise money to pay for the Napoleonic Wars. It was then (and still is) an annual tax which has to be renewed by Parliament each year; nevertheless it has now had an unbroken history since 1842 and there seems little prospect of this changing.

The taxation of capital as opposed to income in the United Kingdom is generally of more recent origin. Thus *capital gains tax* goes back only to 1965, while *inheritance tax* as such came in only in 1986; however, it succeeds earlier taxes in this area dating back to 1894. These two imposts are examined in 1.5 and 1.6 below.

Although not strictly a tax, *national insurance contributions* are an important revenue raiser for the government, and their effect is considered in 1.7.

One other form of tax that should be mentioned is *stamp duty*. At one time a major source of income for the government applying to a very wide range of transactions, it now applies only to certain transactions involving a document evidencing a transfer of ownership. In particular it applies to the following transfers:

(a) *Real property*. The rate of duty is 1% on the consideration, but nothing is charged on sales up to £30,000.
(b) *Stocks and shares*. The rate of duty on most transfers is 0·5% on the consideration.

1.2   INCOME TAX

An individual's income tax liability is always computed by reference to his or her total income from all sources for a *year of assessment* (or *tax year*) ended 5 April, as follows:

Income	X
Less Allowable deductions such as mortgage interest	(X)
Statutory total income	X
Less Personal allowances	(X)
Income chargeable to tax	(X)

This last amount is taxed on a sliding scale; in the current tax year ended 5 April 1988 (referred to as '1987/88'), this scale starts at 27% up to £17,900, rising to a top rate of

60% for chargeable income over £41,200. The full table of rates for 1987/88 is shown at Appendix A.

For historical reasons, different sources of income are taxed in the UK under various headings known as *Schedules*, running from A to F, each with their own special rules, which are looked at below. In addition, most forms of *investment income* are paid, or treated as paid, with income tax deducted at source; these are considered in 1.3.

Certain payments may be deductible for income tax purposes and these are looked at in 1.4, while *personal allowances* are reviewed in 1.4.1.

What follows can be only a brief summary of the position. Readers who feel that they need further advice on any particular aspect are strongly recommended to seek professional advice.

1.2.1 Schedule A

This charges to tax most forms of *income from property* (other than furnished lettings which are usually taxed under Schedule D Case VI, see 1.2.4). The measure of income chargeable to tax is the *rent receivable* in the tax year less *expenses paid*. Rent is brought in as it falls due for collection, and no adjustment is made for rent received late; however, relief is normally allowed for rent which proves to be irrecoverable because of the tenant's default.

Allowable expenses cover the liabilities payable by the landlord under the terms of the lease, such as

- repairs;
- fire insurance;
- agents' charges for collecting rents;
- cleaning and maintenance of common parts (unless recovered from tenants).

The tax is due on 1 January in the tax year concerned. Normally a provisional assessment is made to collect this tax, based on the previous year's figures, and this is adjusted upwards or downwards when the correct figures for the year are known.

1.2.2   Schedule B

This is a largely obsolete tax which now applies only to certain categories of *woodlands* but which can be valuable in the tax planning field.

1.2.3   Schedule C

This is concerned only with the mechanics of collecting tax on certain interest payments made by the British government and by foreign governments in Britain and does not directly affect individual taxpayers at all.

1.2.4   Schedule D

This schedule covers a wide range of sources of income and for convenience is divided into six cases.

CASE I INCOME FROM TRADE
CASE II INCOME FROM PROFESSION OR VOCATION

For all practical purposes, these two cases are identical in operation and are therefore taken together. They operate to tax the profits arising from all forms of *self-employment*, including sole traders, professionals such as doctors, dentists, solicitors and accountants, and individuals carrying on business together in *partnership*.

The amount assessable in a particular tax year is normally taken from the business accounts for the year ended in the preceding tax year (therefore commonly referred to as the 'preceding year basis'). Thus if the business regularly makes up its accounts to 30 April, the amount assessable for the current tax year 1987/88 will be based on the profits of the year to 30 April 1986 (being the accounts year ended in the preceding tax year 1986/87).

Tax is due in two equal instalments, the first on 1 January in the tax year concerned, the second on the following 1 July. Thus in the foregoing example, tax is due for 1987/88 in two instalments on 1 January and 1 July 1988, i.e. 20 months and 26 months respectively after the end of the accounting period concerned. A business is free to choose whatever accounting date it wishes and in many cases this will be influenced by commercial factors, such as the seasonal nature of the business and stock levels; nevertheless choosing an accounting date *early* in the tax year can provide an opportunity for deferring, quite legitimately, tax liabilities on the profits of a particular period.

To enable the assessment of tax to tie in with the *commencement* and *cessation* of a business, special rules apply to the opening and closing years, as follows:

Opening years

First year of assessment	Actual profits from date of commencement to following 5 April (where accounts are not made up to 5 April, the figure would be calculated by time apportionment of the profits of the accounts straddling that date)
Second year of assessment	Profits of first 12 months
Third year of assessment	Profits of accounts ending in preceding year of assessment or of first 12 months

It is open to the taxpayer, if he wishes, to have the assessments of the second and third years of assessment based on the actual profits of those years, again found by time apportionment of the actual accounts. This would be helpful if the profits of the initial years showed a falling trend.

Thereafter the preceding year basis, already explained, applies.

Closing years

Final year of assessment	Actual profits from preceding 6 April to date of cessation

The two immediately preceding years of assessment will follow the normal preceding year basis, except that if it is to its advantage the Inland Revenue may *increase* the assessments of both years to the actual profits of those years.

Special arrangements apply to partnerships, especially where a partner retires or a new partner is admitted, and skilled professional advice is essential.

While the profits for tax purposes are normally derived from those shown in the business accounts, certain differences must be recognized:

(a) *Expenses*. These are allowed provided that they are incurred *wholly and exclusively* for the purpose of earning the profits of the business. This means that expenses incurred partly for business and partly for private purposes are strictly not allowable at all, but in practice it is usually possible to agree a suitable apportionment with the Revenue. Thus where a self-employed individual works from his own home, a reasonable proportion of the outgoings on his house, e.g. rates, light and heat, cleaning, would normally be allowed.

(b) *Entertaining expenses*. There is a specific disallowance for entertaining UK customers or suppliers, though the entertaining of 'overseas customers' and of staff (up to a reasonable level) is allowable. This bar also extends to the making of gifts except at a modest level for limited advertising purposes.

(c) *Personal expenses, drawings, etc.* These are not allowable under any circumstances.

(d) *Capital expenditure.* No deduction as such is allowed for capital expenditure for business purposes or for depreciation of assets as charged in the accounts. Instead, a fixed scale of *capital allowances* is available; the most notable of these are as follows:

- Plant and machinery: 25% on reducing balance each year.
- Motor cars: 25% on reducing balance each year, not exceeding £2,000 for any one car.
- Industrial buildings: 4% on cost each year; except in enterprise zones, where allowances up to 100% may be available, no allowances are given on commercial or office buildings or shops nor in any circumstances on residential property.
- Agricultural buildings: 4% on cost each year.

The various forms of accelerated allowances, known as 'first year allowances' and 'initial allowances', were largely phased out at 31 March 1986.

Special rules apply to make balancing adjustments, which may affect the purchaser as well as the vendor, on the sale of any assets affected by these allowances.

Where a trading or professional business incurs a *loss* for income tax purposes, relief is available in a number of ways:

(a) By being set off against the trader's other income of the same tax year or of the following year, if the business is still continuing.

(b) By being carried forward for set off against future profits of the same business.

(c) Where the loss is incurred in any of the first four tax years in which it is carried on, by being carried back for set off against the trader's other income of the three preceding years, taking the earliest year first (which may therefore be before the business started operating).

(d) Where the loss is incurred in the last 12 months of operation, by being carried back for set off against the profits of the same business in the three preceding years, taking the latest year first.

Further information on the operation of this complex area of taxation, and particularly of the planning opportunities that apply, is contained in *The Touche Ross Tax Guide for the Self-Employed 1987/88* by Bill Packer and Colin Sandy (Papermac, 1987).

CASE III UNTAXED INTEREST

This applies whenever interest is received *gross*, i.e. without any deduction of tax. With the extension of the *composite rate tax* system to banks in 1985 (see 1.3.2) and to local authorities in 1986, it now mainly applies to interest from National Savings Bank accounts.

Here again, tax is charged on a *preceding year* basis, by reference to the interest credited to the individual's account in the preceding tax year ended 5 April. Thus the amount assessable in the current tax year 1987/88 will be the interest credited in the year 1986/87.

Again special rules apply to the opening and closing years, as follows:

Opening years

Year of assessment in which income first arises	Actual interest for that year
Second year of assessment	Actual interest for that year (unless interest first arose on 6 April of preceding year, when preceding year basis applies here)
Third year of assessment	Interest for preceding year, but taxpayer has the option to be assessed on actual

Closing years

Year of assessment in which source ceases (i.e. account is closed)	Actual interest for that year
Year of assessment preceding final year	Preceding year normally applies, but Revenue has the option to increase the assessment to actual

Strictly speaking, each separate source of untaxed interest has to be treated separately according to these rules, but in practice the Revenue will often aggregate these and treat them as one.

Tax is due on 1 January in the year of assessment concerned.

CASE IV INCOME FROM FOREIGN SECURITIES
CASE V INCOME FROM FOREIGN POSSESSIONS

These two cases bring within the charge to UK tax most sources of overseas income, in particular *overseas investment income* which is not subject to UK tax at source and earnings from a *trade or profession carried on wholly abroad*.

The basis of assessment is the same as for Schedule D Case III, so the preceding year basis applies, with adjustments for the opening and closing years, and the tax is due on 1 January in the year of assessment.

While generally the amount of the assessment is based on the income *arising*, irrespective of whether it is paid to the taxpayer in the UK or overseas, a different basis applies if the individual is either *not domiciled* in the UK or, if a British subject or citizen of the Irish Republic, is *not ordinarily resident* in the UK (see 7.3). If either of these situations applies, then the assessment is based on the income *remitted* to the UK in the basis year concerned.

Where this income is subject to overseas tax, for example in the country where it arises, credit for this is normally given against the corresponding liability to UK tax (see 7.7).

CASE VI OTHER INCOME

This is a 'mopping-up' case, intended to pick up those sources of income which are not caught elsewhere in the taxing system. The most common category of income taxed under this head is that from *furnished lettings*. Particularly favourable tax treatment is accorded to the letting of *furnished holiday accommodation*, so that for virtually all income tax and capital gains tax purposes it is treated as a trade.

Tax is normally assessed on the basis of income received less expenses paid in the current tax year, with the tax due on 1 January in the tax year concerned.

1.2.5   Schedule E

This schedule embraces all earnings from *employment*, so as not only to include salaries and wages, but also to extend to directors' remuneration, benefits in kind (see below), termination payments (see Chapter 8), holiday pay, pensions, round sum allowances, share options and many other payments within this general heading.

For most individuals working as employees in the UK, their pay is subject to tax applied by the employer under the Pay-As-You-Earn (PAYE) system. This normally takes account of any allowances and deductions which the employee is entitled to for that tax year, so that the appropriate amount of tax is withheld from his weekly or monthly pay, arriving at the current amount of tax due for the tax year on his pay. For a large number of employees each year, this completes the settlement of their tax liabilities for that year, and no further action is required by them or by the Revenue.

A formal assessment to determine the position for the year may be required where the correct allowances and deductions have not been given through the PAYE system or where it is necessary to adjust for remuneration paid in one year which relates to an earlier year, e.g. bonus or commission.

It is possible for an employee to claim a deduction for *expenses* where he can show that these have been *wholly, exclusively and necessarily incurred in the performance of the duties of the employment*. The inclusion of the test of 'necessity' renders such a claim difficult in practice as far as expenses actually incurred out of the employee's own pocket are concerned, and the problem is normally limited to testing the allowability of expenses reimbursed by the employer where there may be some personal benefit involved.

Contributions to approved pension schemes operated by the employer are always deductible in full; this area is examined in Chapter 4.

A major area of interest is in the widespread use of *benefits in kind* ('fringe benefits' or 'perks') as part of employees' remuneration packages. In principle, the value of any benefits falls to be included as part of an employee's pay from his employment; different rules apply depending on whether the employee is paid at a rate of more or less than £8,500 a year or if he is a director.

For this purpose only, remuneration is calculated to include benefits valued as if he were paid over this threshold and any expenses reimbursed to him by the employer, whether or not they satisfy the 'wholly, exclusively and necessarily incurred' test mentioned earlier.

If the individual's remuneration on this basis is less than a rate of £8,500 a year, any benefits he receives are valued according to the amount, if anything, that he can realize by converting them into money, in effect the 'second-hand' value. As many benefits simply cannot be converted into money in any way, they do not have a taxable value for these purposes.

On the other hand, if the individual is paid at a rate of more than £8,500 a year on this basis (when he is referred to as a 'higher paid employee'), or if he is a director of the employer company, any benefits he receives from the employer are valued by reference to their *cost* to the employer. Special rules have been devised for particular types of benefit: thus the provision of a company car is valued by reference to a scale based on the size, age and cost of the car, with a similar scale where petrol is supplied for private use (see Appendix D).

This is an area of considerable complexity with many opportunities for tax planning for both employers and employees, and also many pitfalls for the unwary. Further information is available in *The Touche Ross Tax Guide to Pay and Perks 1987/88* by Bill Packer and Elaine Baker (Papermac, 1987).

1.2.6   Schedule F

This is concerned with the mechanics of collecting tax on interest and dividend payments made by UK resident companies and does not directly apply to individual taxpayers.

1.3   INVESTMENT INCOME

In the previous section we considered various forms of income which are subject to tax in the UK by direct assessment. As already explained, most forms of investment income are in practice paid, or treated as paid, *net* of income tax, so that the recipient is required to take this into account in his tax settlement for the year.

1.3.1 Interest received

Interest paid on virtually all forms of stocks issued by the UK Government (generally referred to as gilt-edged stocks but not including National Savings investments) is paid with income tax deducted at source at the basic rate of (currently) 27%. Thus the holder of £20,000 3% Treasury Stock 1987 will receive an interest payment on 14 July 1987 as follows:

	£
Half-year's interest £20,000 × 3% × ½	300
Less Income tax at 27%	81
	£219

Three possibilities now apply:

(a) The recipient is liable only to tax at the basic rate. This income is therefore regarded as fully taxed and no further action is required apart from a requirement to include it in his tax return.
(b) The recipient has unrelieved personal allowances or other deductions. He can reclaim tax on such allowances up to £300 on each such payment by producing the voucher that accompanies the interest

payment. Normally this can be done only after the end of the tax year concerned.

(c) If the recipient's total income is such that he is liable to tax at rates above the basic rate, then an assessment to collect the additional tax (known as 'excess liability') will be raised after the end of the tax year. Suppose the recipient's top rate of tax for 1987/88 is 60%; the excess liability on this interest received would be determined as follows:

Interest received	£300
Income tax thereon at 60%	180
Less Basic rate tax already deducted at 27%	81
Excess liability	£99

This tax is due on 1 December following the end of the year of assessment concerned (i.e. 1 December 1988) or 30 days after the issue of the notice of assessment, whichever is later.

The same rules apply to interest paid by companies on loan and debenture stocks and similar fixed rate securities (but not preference shares; see 1.3.3).

1.3.2   Bank and building society interest received

The arrangements set out in 1.3.1 are modified as regards interest received from building societies and from bank deposit accounts maintained at banks in the UK. These bodies operate a special system known as *composite rate tax*; this has applied to building societies for many years and to banks since 6 April 1985.

The main difference so far as a recipient of such interest is concerned is that although the interest is still regarded as paid under deduction of income tax at the basic rate, the recipient, where he is otherwise entitled to do so (see paragraph (b) in 1.3.1), cannot reclaim any of this tax. This therefore makes such an account a bad investment for the non-taxpayer.

It is possible for an entity such as a charity, which is not liable to income tax at all, or for an individual who is not ordinarily resident (see 7.3), to apply to his bank or building society to have the interest paid gross.

1.3.3 Dividends received from UK companies

When a company resident in the UK pays a dividend, it is required to account to the Inland Revenue for advance corporation tax ('ACT') on that dividend. This is used as a payment in advance of the company's liability to corporation tax on the profits of the period in which the dividend is paid. This arrangement applies to fixed rate holdings, such as preference shares, as well as to ordinary shares.

It is also treated as a 'tax credit' in the hands of each recipient and is exactly equivalent to income tax at the basic rate on the dividend paid plus the tax credit.

To illustrate this in figures, if the company pays out a

dividend of £73,000 in July 1987, it will have to account for ACT of 27/73rds of £73,000, i.e. £27,000. It will be seen that £27,000 is 27% (current basic rate of income tax) of £73,000 + £27,000.

If a shareholder receives, as part of this distribution, a dividend of £73, he will have an associated tax credit of £27. In effect he will be treated as receiving a 'gross' equivalent dividend of £100 with tax deemed to be deducted of £27; then the other consequences set out in 1.3.1 will follow. The difference in treatment is purely technical and is of no practical consequence to an individual recipient.

The position of overseas residents is looked at in 7.7.2.

1.3.4   Dividends received from overseas companies

Where a dividend is received by the shareholder direct from an overseas company, it will be liable to tax by assessment under Schedule D Case V (see 1.2.4).

However, it is common practice for such dividends to be collected on the shareholder's behalf by his bank or other paying agent. In this case, the agent deducts income tax at the basic rate from the payment received, so that the shareholder receives his dividend *net* instead of *gross*. It would then be treated in the same way as interest payments described in 1.3.1.

Where the dividend is subject to a withholding tax in the country of origin, the agent will normally give relief for this in the income tax deduction that he makes.

1.4 DEDUCTIONS

1.4.1 Personal allowances

For 1986/87 the lower personal allowance was £2,335; for 1987/88 it is £2,425. This is given to an unmarried person (whether single, divorced or widowed), and even if the taxpayer is not entitled to claim any other allowances, this amount will be deducted from his income before the tax is calculated.

There is a higher personal allowance for a married man whose wife lives with him, or is wholly maintained by him. There are special rules for the year of marriage or separation (see Chapters 2 and 9). The relief for 1986/87 was £3,655 and for 1987/88 it is £3,795.

These allowances are normally adjusted each year at least in line with inflation.

Tax allowances in respect of children were generally abolished some years ago; there is, however, an *additional personal allowance* which may be claimed by a single parent in certain circumstances and this is looked at in 9.2.2. The allowances have been replaced by child benefits which are payable direct to the mother of the child (to the father if he is responsible for bringing up the child) by the Department of Health and Social Security normally through the Post Office or by credit transfer. These child benefits are not taxable.

The status of 'common law wife' is not recognized for tax purposes.

There are several other reliefs which an individual may be able to claim; these are noted below.

Dependent relative. The dependant must be a relative who is maintained by the claimant, and must be incapacitated by old age or infirmity, unless she is the mother of the claimant, or his wife, when the only test is that she is widowed, divorced or separated. ('Relative' includes a relative of either husband or wife.)

The allowance is £100 a year but this is increased to £145 for a woman claimant other than a married woman living with her husband. To obtain the full allowance the relative's income must not exceed the basic retirement pension for the year in question – the allowance is reduced by £1 for every £1 the relative's income exceeds this limit.

If the relative is not living with the claimant, the allowance will be given, as a concession, if his contribution is £75 or more each year.

Daughter's or son's services. The daughter or son must be resident with the claimant and be maintained by him. He must be compelled to depend on their services because of old age or infirmity. The allowance is £55 a year.

Blind person's relief. This can be claimed by a single person or a married man if he or his wife is registered as blind throughout the whole or part of the year. If both spouses are blind, the allowance is given twice. The allowance is £540 a year.

Housekeeper allowance. A claim for this allowance (£100) can be made by a widow or widower but not by a person who is divorced or separated, in respect of a relative who is resident with the claimant or an unrelated person who is resident and employed as a housekeeper. This is no longer a common relief because if there are children involved there is an additional personal allowance that may be claimed (see 9.2.2).

Life assurance relief. For most life assurance policies issued up to and including 13 March 1984, income tax relief at 15% is allowed on the premiums paid. Normally the relief is given by deduction by the payer from the premiums he pays, so that no intervention is required by the tax office.

The relief is not given on policies issued after 13 March 1984; it will also be withdrawn on any existing policies made before that date if the policy terms are altered so as to improve the benefits received.

1.4.2   Interest paid

Interest on loans for the purchase, improvement or development of land, including buildings, in the UK or the Republic of Ireland, but not the Channel Islands, is specifically allowable for tax purposes, provided certain conditions are met.

At the time the interest is paid the property must be the sole or main residence of the borrower, a dependent relative of the borrower (or his or her spouse) living there rent free, or a separated spouse. The loan must be used for the purposes of purchasing or improving the house, and not just by way of borrowing capital using the house as security. The relief is limited to interest on the first £30,000 of the loan. Also allowable for income tax purposes is a bridging loan taken out for the purchase of one residence with a view to the previous residence being sold; again the relief is limited to the first £30,000 of the loan. (See also 10.4.)

In any case tax relief can be claimed only on the interest element of mortgage payments and not on capital repayments.

For most individuals, with effect from 6 April 1983, tax relief for interest paid is given through the *mortgage interest relief at source* ('MIRAS') scheme. Under this arrangement income tax at the basic rate (at present 27%) is withheld by the borrower from the gross interest due and only the *net* amount is paid to the lender.

If the borrower is a basic rate taxpayer, once the net payment has been made there is no further tax relief due. However, if he is liable to pay tax at the higher rates he is entitled to further relief which will normally be given in his PAYE coding or against a Schedule D or other direct assessment.

There is no tax relief for interest charged on overdrafts or credit cards (or similar arrangements), unless it is incurred wholly and exclusively for the purposes of the taxpayer's business as a sole trader or partner and is charged directly in his business accounts.

Loan interest relief will also be allowed if the money is borrowed for any of the following purposes:

(a) A loan to purchase or improve property which is let at a commercial rent for at least 26 weeks of the year and when not being let is available to be let or undergoing repair. (There may be some restrictions as to the relief available.)

(b) Provision is also made to cover the situation where the borrower is living in accommodation provided by the employer as one of the requirements of his job, but at the same time the employee is paying interest on a loan to buy a house which he is either using as a residence at the time or intends to so use within 12 months; this allows relief to be claimed for interest paid by the employee on a loan on a house bought in anticipation of moving out of his present 'job-related' living accommodation. A similar relief is available where the individual is self-employed and is required to live in 'job-related' accommodation. (Relief on maximum £30,000 loan only.)

(c) A loan for purchase of plant or machinery for use in a trade if the borrower is a partner in the business, or for use in the borrower's office or employment. Relief is granted only in the tax year in which the loan is taken out and the following three years, and only if a claim for capital allowances on the plant and machinery has been granted.

(d) A loan for purchase of ordinary shares in, or making a loan to, a close company, subject to certain conditions.

(e) A loan for purchase of a share in, or making a loan to, a partnership. The lender must be a member of the partnership; where the money is lent to the partnership it must be used for the purposes of the partnership business.

(f) A loan to make payment of capital transfer tax, estate duty or inheritance tax in respect of a deceased person. The relief is granted to the personal representatives for a period of one year only from the date of the loan.

(g) A loan up to £30,000 to purchase a life annuity by a borrower, male or female, aged 65 or over. He or she must use his or her own home as security for the loan, and at least 90% of the proceeds of the loan must be used to purchase the annuity. The limit for the loan to qualify is again £30,000. See also 4.14.

(h) A loan to buy shares in an 'employee-controlled company'; this can arise where employees as a group are given the opportunity to buy a controlling interest in an unquoted company from its existing proprietors (this again may be subject to some restrictions, depending mainly on the percentage shareholding acquired by the individual).

1.4.3 Deeds of covenant

The use of deeds of covenant as a form of tax planning is now widely familiar. It turns on a *donor* (the *covenantor*) undertaking for a defined period to make a *gratuitous transfer* of income (thus there must be no consideration passing) to a *donee* (the *beneficiary*). The donor withholds income tax at the basic rate from the payments he makes, thus gaining a measure of tax relief. The donee is regarded as receiving income which has been taxed at source: if he is not a taxpayer, either because he does not have enough income to cover his personal allowances or because of being exempt as a charity, he can reclaim that tax. Thus the gift costs the donor no more than the *net* amount; the donee is able to have the benefit of the *gross* amount.

Deeds of covenant now fall into two categories, charitable and non-charitable, with somewhat different rules:

Charitable covenants. The deed must be for a period *capable of exceeding three years.* The donor is normally entitled to higher rate tax relief on the total gross amount paid except that there may be some restriction to this where the charity concerned is not able to meet fully the current more stringent conditions for charitable exemption. This whole area of charitable giving is looked at in more detail in 10.5.

Non-charitable covenants. Where the donee is not a charity, the deed must be for a period *capable of exceeding six years* (hence the familiar 'seven-year covenant'). In this case, the donor does not get any higher rate tax relief but the donee may still be able to reclaim the basic rate tax deducted. This is a particularly useful tool within the context of family tax planning and is looked at further in 2.6.3, 3.2 and 7.3.3.

1.4.4 Maintenance payments

Maintenance payments in connection with the breakdown of a marriage are generally made using the same mechanics as already described for loan interest paid under MIRAS (see 1.4.2) and charitable covenants (see 1.4.3).

Thus the payer deducts tax at the basic rate from the payments he makes and should also be entitled, if applicable, to higher rate tax relief. Correspondingly, the payee is treated as receiving income *net* of tax so that she may be entitled to an income tax repayment to cover personal allowances or other deductions. An exception to this treatment is that given to *small maintenance payments* (as defined; see 9.2.6) which are always made gross.

The tax implications of separation and divorce generally are considered in Chapter 9.

1.5   CAPITAL GAINS TAX

1.5.1   Introduction

Capital gains tax, normally abbreviated to 'CGT' and first introduced on 6 April 1965, is a completely separate tax from income tax. The basis of charge to this tax is as follows: when a chargeable person, resident or ordinarily resident in the UK (see 7.3), disposes of a chargeable asset, either a chargeable gain or an allowable loss will arise.

In simple terms there is a chargeable gain if the net proceeds received on disposal of an asset exceed the total cost of the asset at the date it was acquired. Similarly, if the proceeds on disposal are less than the cost of the asset at acquisition, an allowable loss will arise.

This was substantially affected by the introduction, with effect from 6 April 1982 (1 April for companies), of an allowance known as *indexation*; this was further modified with effect from 6 April 1985 (again 1 April for companies). What follows in 1.5.2 describes the operation of the relief from the latter dates.

As for income tax, husband and wife are treated as one person for CGT purposes (but see 2.6.2).

Death is *not* an occasion for charge to CGT.

1.5.2 Indexation allowance

The indexation allowance adjustment added to the cost of the asset represents the increase in the retail prices index (RPI) from the date that it was acquired to the date of the sale so as to reduce the gain or increase the loss. If the asset was acquired before April 1982, the increase in the index is measured from 31 March 1982 and applied to the cost of the asset or its market value at that date if this was greater than its cost. These rules are illustrated in these examples:

(a) An asset purchased in June 1982 and disposed of in May 1987 will qualify for the indexation allowance applied to original cost by reference to the increase in the RPI from June 1982 to May 1987.

(b) An asset purchased in August 1981 and disposed of in May 1987 will qualify for the indexation allowance applied to original cost or if greater its market value at 31 March 1982 by reference to the increase in the RPI from that date to May 1987.

For disposals prior to April 1985, the indexation relief was somewhat more limited, the main differences being as follows:

(a) There was a 'waiting period' of 12 months from acquisition before the allowance applied.

(b) For acquisitions prior to April 1982, the allowance was applied only to original cost.

(c) It was available only to reduce or extinguish gains and did not apply to losses at all.

1.5.3 Annual exemption

There is an annual exemption in each tax year. For 1987/88 this has been fixed at £6,600. As with the personal allowances for income tax (see 1.4.1), this exemption is normally adjusted each year in line with inflation.

It may therefore be possible to achieve some savings of tax by spreading disposals over several tax years so as to make full use of the annual exemptions.

Where the chargeable gains do exceed the exemption limit in any tax year, tax is payable at 30% on the excess.

For trusts, the exemption limit is half that for individuals, i.e. £3,300 for 1987/88; again tax is payable at 30% on the excess. There is no corresponding exemption for companies.

1.5.4 Losses

Losses on the disposal of assets can be set against gains arising on the disposal of other assets in the same tax year or carried forward to set off against gains arising in later years. There is generally no provision for carrying back losses to earlier years; the only exception to this is that where there are unrelieved losses in the year of death (when there is no means by which they may be carried forward), they may be carried back to set off against gains incurred in the preceding three tax years.

Where losses are brought forward from earlier years, they are set off against gains of a current year, only to the extent that these are reduced to the amount of the exemption for the year; any balance is then carried forward.

1.5.5   Exempt assets

Gains arising on the disposal of certain assets, as set out below, are exempt from capital gains tax; by the same token any loss arising on their disposal is not allowable for these purposes.

Principal private residence. When the property is disposed of, there are no capital gains tax consequences provided the property has been the individual's only or main residence. This will include land of up to one acre, though where it is required for the reasonable enjoyment of the residence having regard to its size and character this area may be increased. (See also 10.4.)

Where a second home is acquired, an election should be submitted to the Inland Revenue stating which is to be the principal private residence. Where no election is submitted the Inspector of Taxes has powers to determine which property to consider the principal private residence based on the particular facts, but the Inspector's decision is subject to appeal. There can be only one principal private residence for a married couple living together.

Any gains realized on a disposal of a private residence occupied by a dependent relative of the individual or of his spouse is also tax free provided that it is a sole residence of the dependant and that the property is provided rent free and without any other consideration. The payment of normal tenants' expenses such as rates will not harm entitlement to this exemption.

Where a property was acquired wholly or partly for the purpose of realizing a gain on its disposal no relief will be available, and there is even the possibility that the Revenue may argue in such cases that the owner has been trading in land.

In the situation where a residence has been occupied as the individual's main residence for a part only of the period of ownership any gain arising has to be apportioned in accordance with special rules. These rules also come into play where part of the house is being used exclusively for business purposes. Where part of the property has been let, the proportion of the gain attributable to the let part of the property is taxable only to the extent that it exceeds £20,000 or the exempt proportion of the gain attributable to the owner-occupied part, whichever is the lesser amount.

Where the property is not occupied for certain specified reasons the capital gains tax exemption need not be lost. These exemptions include:

(a) any part of the last 24 months of ownership;
(b) a one-year delay by the owner-occupier in taking up residence;
(c) general absences not exceeding three years;
(d) absence up to four years connected with employment;
(e) other absences arising out of working overseas.

Chattels. These are assets which are touchable ('tangible') and movable. They are exempt if the disposal is for £3,000 or less. (A special computation is necessary if the sum marginally exceeds £3,000.) This does not apply to currency (but see under 'Foreign currency' below). There are also special rules dealing with 'sets' of chattels.

Wasting assets. Chattels (see above) which have an expected life of less than 50 years (e.g. a yacht or a racehorse) are exempt from CGT. Other wasting assets (e.g. a short lease of a property) are subject to special rules.

Motor cars. These are not chargeable assets unless they are of a type not commonly used as a private vehicle and unsuitable to be so used.

National Savings certificates, premium bonds, etc. These are always exempt whenever they are acquired or disposed of.

Government securities ('gilt-edged'). These are exempt as regards disposals made on or after 2 July 1986; previously the exemption applied only if the stock had been held for more than 12 months. A similar exemption applies to certain fixed interest loan stocks issued after 13 March 1984.

It should be noted, however, that any accrued interest received on or after 28 February 1986 as part of sale proceeds of such securities does now have to be recognized as the recipient's income and charged to income tax accordingly. A corresponding deduction from his income is allowed to the buyer of the securities. This so-called *accrued interest scheme* does not apply if the individual making the disposal holds securities of this kind with a total nominal value of £5,000 or less throughout both the year of assessment in which the sale took place and the previous one.

Betting and other winnings. Betting winnings are not chargeable gains and rights to winnings obtained by any pool betting or lottery are not chargeable assets. Premium bonds are also exempt.

Foreign currency. Exempt provided it was acquired only for personal and family expenditure.

Medals and decorations. Exempt unless acquired by purchase.

Compensation for damages. Exempt if received for personal or professional wrong or injury; if the damages, etc. relate to an asset, payment will constitute a disposal.

Life assurance policies and deferred annuities. Exempt when disposed of or realized by the original policyholder but not when disposed of or realized by another person who may have acquired them by subsequent purchase.

1.5.6   Holdover relief

If the gift is not exempt the chargeable gain will be assessed as if the asset concerned had been sold for its open-market value, and the person making the gift, i.e. the donor, would normally pay the capital gains tax due accordingly.

From 6 April 1980 if the gift is made to an individual resident in the UK the gain can be held over. This means that instead of the donor paying the tax, the gain will be deducted from the acquisition value of the gift; this in turn means that the donee, i.e. the person receiving the gift, will pay the capital gains tax (subject to any exemptions that he may be able to claim) when the asset is eventually sold, as he has a lower acquisition value to be deducted from the sale proceeds, leaving a higher chargeable gain. Both the donee and the donor must elect jointly for this relief to apply.

Beware, however, if the donee becomes not resident in the UK within six years of the end of the tax year in which the gift was made and he still has the asset, the held-over liability becomes immediately payable. Furthermore, if it cannot get it from the donee, the Inland Revenue has power to tax the donor.

Holdover relief is also available for gifts made to a trust, and for assets transferred out of a trust, for example to a beneficiary.

A useful point to remember (although perhaps rather macabre) is that, as death is not an occasion of charge for capital gains tax purposes, if an asset is given to a donee who subsequently dies and both parties signed an election for this relief to apply, there will be no capital gains tax to pay on that gift. The same result would follow if the asset gifted is a house which then becomes the donee's principal private residence (see 10.4).

1.5.7 Retirement relief

This is a very useful relief which is available to be set against the capital gain arising on the disposal of a business. This can include the disposal of an interest in a partnership or of shares in a family trading company. The disposal of part of a business may also qualify for relief.

The main conditions which need to be satisfied before retirement relief is available are:

(a) the individual must have reached the age of 60 years (male or female) or be retiring early through ill-health; *and*

(b) he must be disposing of the whole or part of a business which he owns or shares in a family trading company of which he is a full-time working director.

The maximum relief of up to £125,000 (for disposals on or before 5 April 1987, the limit was £100,000) is available where (b) is satisfied throughout a period of ten years ending with the disposal. Although strictly the individual must have carried on the business or have been a full-time working director throughout the ten years to comply, relief will still be available where separate businesses are owned in succession. The ten-year rule is also regarded as satisfied where initially the individual carries on the trade personally and subsequently becomes a full-time director of a family company which takes over the trade.

Where the ten-year requirement is not met the relief is reduced on a percentage scale dropping from 100% for ten years to 10% for one year. These conditions must be satisfied for at least one year for any relief to be available.

A detailed commentary on these provisions is contained in *The Touche Ross Tax Guide for the Self-Employed 1987/88* by Bill Packer and Colin Sandy (Papermac, 1987).

1.5.8 Roll-over relief

Although outside the scope of this book, this relief is mentioned here briefly for the sake of completeness. More detailed information is available in *The Touche Ross Tax Guide for the Self-Employed 1987/88*.

As the business develops, assets used for business purposes may from time to time have to be replaced or new ones acquired. In such a situation it is quite likely that, due to the effects of inflation, a chargeable gain may arise. If such gains were taxed in full this would bleed money away from the business which would then not be able to reinvest, and its ability to expand would be restricted. However, provided certain conditions are met, the tax code allows any resulting capital gains tax liability to be deferred. A trader disposing of qualifying assets used exclusively for the purposes of his trade who spends all or part of the proceeds on other assets used in the same way may elect to defer any capital gains tax arising by deducting the chargeable gain from the cost of the new assets. To qualify, expenditure on the new asset must be incurred one year before or three years after disposal of the old assets.

Only the following classes of assets may qualify for roll-over relief:

(a) Land and buildings *occupied* (as well as *used*) only for the purposes of the trade.
(b) Fixed plant and machinery which does not form part of a building.
(c) Ships, aircraft and hovercraft.
(d) Goodwill.

Both the old and new assets must fall within the above classes but need not necessarily be of the same class.

1.6   INHERITANCE TAX

1.6.1   Introduction

Assets passing at death have been subject to various forms of taxation since estate duty was introduced in 1894. This taxed only assets passing on death and certain lifetime gifts, but capital gains tax also applied on death between 1965 and 1971.

In 1974 capital transfer tax was introduced as a wide ranging tax on gifts made during lifetime and on assets passing on death on a cumulative basis. Special provisions were also brought in to tax various forms of trust.

In his Budget speech on 18 March 1986, the Chancellor of the Exchequer introduced a number of radical changes to the existing scheme, including changing its name to *inheritance tax*. The detailed provisions are included in the 1986 and 1987 Finance Acts.

The new tax, which came into operation on 18 March 1986, applies generally to assets passing on death and on gifts made within seven years before death. Certain other categories of lifetime gifts may also be subject to the tax and these are considered at 1.6.2.

Gifts made up to seven years before death will be included with the assets passing at death at their value at the date of the gift, but using the rates of tax in force at the date of death. However, only gifts made up to three years before the death will be included in full; for earlier gifts a form of tapering relief will be available so that only a proportion of the full charge will apply.

Details of the tax rates and of the tapering relief are shown in Appendix B.

1.6.2 Tax-free gifts

In general for gifts made on or after 18 March 1986 other than those caught by the 'seven-year' charge mentioned in 1.6.1 there will be no charge to tax on lifetime gifts made between individuals and into certain 'qualifying' trusts (see 1.6.5): such gifts are referred to as *potentially exempt transfers* ('PETs'). However, a charge will be made on gifts into discretionary trusts made at any time. The rates applicable will be half those that would be applied using the table in Appendix B.

The above applies where a 'gift' is clearly that, namely a free and unencumbered transfer of an asset. However, special rules apply where the gift is not made outright; technically this is referred to as a *gift with reservation* and would apply where the donor continues to enjoy some benefit from the gifted asset. An example of this would be where an individual gives his house to another member of the family, subject to him (the donor) continuing to live in it rent free. In such a case the gift would be treated as made only when the reservation is released or the enjoyment finally ceases. In this example of the house already mentioned, this could apply when the donor moved out to live elsewhere, giving up his rights of occupation, or perhaps on his death. If the gift is thus treated as taking place on the donor's death or within a period of seven years before, inheritance tax will apply as described in 1.6.1.

Husband and wife. Unlike income tax and capital gains tax, a husband and wife are treated as separate individuals for inheritance tax purposes. Furthermore a transfer between husband and wife is generally exempt from tax, with one exception. Where the spouse receiving the gift is domiciled outside the UK (as defined below), only the first £55,000 would be exempt; any balance may therefore come within the 'seven-year' charge described above.

Domicile. Where an individual is domiciled in the UK he will be liable to pay inheritance tax on all assets irrespective of where they are situated. An individual domiciled abroad will pay tax only on assets that are situated in the UK. The meaning of 'domicile' is discussed in general terms at 7.3.1 but this is extended for inheritance tax purposes. In many situations it is possible to be regarded as domiciled in the UK for inheritance tax purposes even if for other purposes it is accepted that the individual has abandoned or never adopted a United Kingdom domicile. An individual will be caught in this way where:

(a)   he was domiciled under general law in the UK during the three years immediately preceding the making of a gift or death; *or*

(b)   he was resident in the UK in not less than 17 of the
      last 20 tax years ending with the fiscal year in which
      the gift or death falls.

There are certain other categories of lifetime transfers
which are either not chargeable or partially exempt from
a charge to tax; these reliefs are not available on death.

Annual exemption. The first £3,000 of transfers each year is
exempt; any unused relief can be carried forward for one
year only against transfers in excess of the limit for the
later year. Unless there is a regular pattern of making gifts
so that these take place at least every other year some of
the benefit of this exemption may be lost.

Small gifts. The first £250 of transfers to any one individual
in each tax year is exempt. Unused relief cannot be used
in a later year; the exemption applies only to outright gifts,
not to settlements. This is in addition to the annual
exemption mentioned above. It is therefore possible to
pay any number of people £250 in a year and not have
made a chargeable transfer. However, the relief cannot be
used to cover the first slice of a large gift; thus a transfer
of £1,000 would be covered by the annual exemption,
leaving £2,000 available to cover other gifts in the same
year, but could not be covered by the £250 small gifts
exemption so as to use only £750 of the annual exemption.

Gifts in consideration of marriage. Transfers made in consideration of marriage are exempt, but only within set limits
which vary according to the degree of affinity between the

transferor and the parties to the marriage. If the transferor is a parent of one of the parties of the marriage, he may give £5,000; if the transferor is a more remote ancestor he may give £2,500; if the transferee is one of the parties to the marriage the limit is again £2,500; anyone else may give £1,000. For this exemption to be obtained it is important to ensure that there is evidence that the gift is actually made in consideration of the marriage. The gift should be completed before the marriage; unless special steps are taken, such a gift cannot effectively be made after the marriage. Also, in order to comply fully, the gift should be recoverable should the marriage not take place, otherwise the Revenue does not consider that the gift was made *in consideration* of the marriage.

Normal expenditure out of income. If a transfer is effected out of income it may not be relevant for inheritance tax purposes. To qualify for this exemption, the Revenue must be satisfied as to the following three conditions:

(a)   The transfer is made as part of the normal expenditure of the transferor.

(b)   The transfer is made out of his income (comparing one year with another).

(c)   After allowing for all such transfers the transferor is left with a sufficient income to maintain his usual standard of living.

The expenditure must be 'habitual' and the Revenue will look for a pattern of payments made to the same person. The expenditure must involve cash outlay; gifts of assets will qualify only if they were bought for the purpose of making the gift. 'Income' is taken as net of income tax for these purposes.

The following transfers are exempt from tax both as lifetime gifts and on death:

Charities. Transfers to charities, whether during the donor's lifetime or by his will on his death, are wholly exempt from inheritance tax.

Political parties. If a donation is made to a political party, this will be exempt from inheritance tax as a lifetime transfer. However, transfers in excess of £100,000 made on death or within 12 months prior to death are taxable. A political party qualifies only if it has two MPs or if it has one MP and gained 150,000 votes at the last general election.

National heritage. There are three different exemptions in this category:

(a) *Gifts for national purposes*. The transfer is exempt if it becomes the property of specified bodies – certain museums, galleries and trust funds are specified by name, e.g. the National Trust; similar national institutions may be approved by the Treasury; many museums and art galleries maintained by local authorities and Government departments are also included.

(b) *Gifts for public benefit*. The transfer is exempt if it is property which then becomes the property of a non-profit-making organization, provided that the Treasury gives its consent. The property so transferred may be land, buildings, works of art, etc. and the Treasury will be looking for items of outstanding scenic, historic, scientific, architectural or aesthetic value, as appropriate. The Treasury may require undertakings to be given to preserve the asset and to provide reasonable access to the public.

(c) *Conditional exemption.* The property involved in this relief is basically the same as for gifts for the public benefit. The transfer is conditionally exempt to the extent it is attributable to property designated by the Treasury. The property remains in private ownership and the Treasury will require various undertakings to be given before the exemption is allowed. Inheritance tax becomes payable if there is a breach in the conditions or if the property is sold, unless the undertakings are renewed.

Excluded property. Such property is not included in an individual's estate either for the purpose of lifetime transfers or in the event of death. Excluded property includes the following:

(a) property situated outside the UK if the beneficial owner is domiciled abroad (but remembering the special definition of 'domicile' used for inheritance tax purposes mentioned above);

(b) reversionary interest, i.e. something which reverts to an individual, e.g. the right to obtain the capital held in a settlement on the death of the person currently enjoying the income from it. The exclusion does not apply if the interest has been purchased by the individual to whom it will now revert;

(c) certain government securities beneficially owned by persons not domiciled (as generally defined) or habitually resident in the UK;

(d) National Savings owned by persons domiciled (as generally defined) in the Channel Islands or Isle of Man;

(e) property passing as a result of death on active service;

(f) cash options under approved annuity schemes;

(g) overseas pensions;

(h) property owned by a member of visiting armed forces.

1.6.3 Business reliefs

Business property relief. Basically this relief provides that if 'relevant business property' is transferred the value chargeable to inheritance tax will be reduced by a percentage which will vary depending on the type of business property concerned. The relief can be claimed where the transfer is made during lifetime or at death. There is no limit to the value transferred which can qualify for this relief.

Relevant business property includes:

(a) a business or interest in a business (value reduction 50%);

(b) shares or securities in a company which was controlled by the transferor immediately before the transfer (value reduction 50%);

(c)   (for transfers made on or after 17 March 1987) share-holdings of more than 25% in an unquoted company (value reduction 50%);

(d)   other non-controlling shareholdings in an unquoted company (value reduction 30%);

(e)   in certain circumstances, land or buildings, machinery and plant used for business purposes (value reduction 30%).

There are a number of conditions which need to be satisfied both at the time of the gift and at the date of death: the most important of these are that the transferor must have owned the property for at least two years prior to the date of the gift and the transferee must still hold the property at the date of death.

Agricultural property relief. This relief applies to transfers made during lifetime or on death and provides that if the value transferred is attributable to the agricultural value of agricultural property in the UK, occupied by working farmers for a period of two years prior to the transfer, the value may be reduced by 50% of the agricultural value, i.e. excluding any value attributable to possible non-agricultural use.

Where the land is let, for transfers made after 15 March 1983, the landlord may claim a reduction of 30% of the agricultural value.

To qualify for relief, the land must have been occupied by the transferor for agricultural purposes for at least two years before the date of the gift or the date of death *or* owned by him for at least seven years before those dates and occupied by him or by someone else for agricultural purposes throughout that period.

Relief for woodlands. A claim can be made that the value of trees or underwood growing on land in the UK (which is not agricultural property) be left out of account in determining the value transferred on the owner's death. The relief is to be claimed, by the person who would be liable to pay the tax, during the two years following the death, but this time limit may be extended.

The basic condition to be satisfied is that the woodlands must have been owned by the deceased for five years prior to his death or have been acquired by gift or inheritance. There will be no charge to tax unless the woodlands are disposed of either by sale or gift, so it is possible to extend the relief through a succession of deaths. Provided the usual conditions are met an alternative may be to claim business property relief instead and to pay tax on a reduced chargeable value.

Voidable transfers. Inheritance tax is repayable in respect of any transfer which is subsequently declared void by an enactment or rule of law, e.g. bankruptcy.

1.6.4 Valuation of estate

The most likely time when an estate is valued is at the death of the owner. The estate will include all the property of whatever description to which the owner was beneficially entitled. An exception to this rule is life assurance policies which are included in the estate at their full value. At death the estate will also generally include all property contained in a settlement if the deceased had an interest in the capital or income of the trust.

Generally speaking, assets passing are valued at their open-market value at that time, and for most items this is relatively easy to determine, where required, with the help of expert valuers. One particular area of difficulty lies in the valuation of *unquoted shares*, where there are usually major restrictions on the transfer of the shares outside, say, the family or the immediate shareholding group and there is effectively no such thing as an open market. Following a line of court cases, a body of practice has grown up between the Inland Revenue and share valuation specialists in the accountancy field whereby an agreed valuation can be arrived at in what are essentially hypo-thetical circumstances. Specialist professional advice is essential in this area.

1.6.5   Settlements

The use of settlements as a form of tax planning has always attracted considerable attention from the legislators, and settlements of all kinds are specially treated for inheritance tax purposes. As mentioned in 1.6.2, gifts into certain trusts qualify as potentially exempt transfers in the same way as gifts between individuals, i.e. a charge to inherit-ance tax arises only if the transferor dies within seven years of making the gift. The trusts which are treated in this way are accumulation and maintenance settlements, trusts for the disabled and (with effect from 17 March 1987) interest in possession settlements; these are described in more detail in 5.2, but the rules are summarized here for the sake of completeness.

Where the trust is what is called *discretionary*, so that there is no one entitled to any part of the income or capital of the trust, tax at half the normal rates is chargeable on the transfer into the settlement. In addition, a special charge to tax at reduced rates is levied on the assets of the trust every ten years or when any assets are transferred out, for example to a beneficiary.

Special treatment is given to the following types of settlement:

Accumulation and maintenance settlement. The following conditions must all be met:

(a) One or more persons will become entitled to an 'interest in possession' (which may be absolute ownership or need be only an interest in the income) on or before attaining the age of 25 years.
(b) Income is accumulated unless used for the maintenance, education or benefit of a beneficiary.
(c) Not more than 25 years have elapsed since the creation of the settlement or all beneficiaries are grandchildren of a common grandparent.

If the trust qualifies, no tax will arise on gifts made into it more than seven years before the settlor's death; the periodic charge mentioned above for discretionary trusts will not be payable and no further tax will arise when a beneficiary attains his interest.

Interest in possession settlement. This is a form of trust where there are one or more beneficiaries entitled to share in the income. With effect from 17 March 1987, transfers into such settlements are exempt from inheritance tax provided that the settlor survives seven years. A similar potential exemption applies when a beneficiary's interest comes to an end, provided that the interest in the trust assets passes to another individual or to another qualifying trust and provided that the beneficiary survives for at least seven years after the ceasing of his interest.

Otherwise the assets of the trust are treated as part of the beneficiary's estate for inheritance tax purposes at his death.

Protective trust. This would come into force in the instance where the principal beneficiary attempts to assign his interest to someone else. This would give the trustees discretion over the income but the periodic charge already referred to would not be payable even on the subsequent death of the principal beneficiary.

Trust for the disabled. There is no tax payable if the trust is created for a disabled person more than seven years before the donor's death. Where the beneficiary is mentally disabled, any periodic charges are deferred until his death.

Charitable trust. Trusts which are wholly charitable are not subject to a tax on entry and they are exempt from the periodic charge and from tax on all distributions.

Employee trust. For trusts of this type to qualify the beneficiaries must be restricted to persons of a class defined by reference to employment, persons married to those so defined, or charities. Payments to beneficiaries are not classed as capital distributions, except in special circumstances, and the periodic charge is deferred until a capital distribution payment is made.

1.6.6 Paying the tax

Tax is usually due within 12 months of the end of the month in which the death occurred, but interest at 6% will be payable after six months. The persons primarily responsible for paying the tax are the personal representatives, but the Inland Revenue does have power to follow the liability through to any person in whom the property passing is vested after death. In the case of a lifetime gift which is caught, the tax attributable to that gift is normally collectable from the recipient unless there is special provision in the donor's will allowing it to be charged against his estate.

Where any tax has already been paid on a gift, for example under the previous rules applicable to capital transfer tax, this will be allowed as a credit against the corresponding tax arising on the death.

If the necessary funds to pay the tax are not available, the Revenue may accept any of the following property as a payment in kind: land; buildings, and contents associated with those buildings; pictures, prints, books, manuscripts, works of art, scientific objects or items, or collections of such items, if of national, scientific, historic or artistic interest.

1.7   NATIONAL INSURANCE CONTRIBUTIONS

The Social Security Acts provide for a range of benefits to be paid to individuals in return for the payment of national insurance contributions by them and, where appropriate, their employer, towards the cost of providing these benefits.

There are four classes of contribution:

- Class 1 *primary*: earnings related and payable by employees; *secondary*: earnings related and payable by employers in respect of their employees. These contributions are collected through the PAYE system.
- Class 2 – flat rate contribution payable weekly by people in self-employment.
- Class 3 – voluntary contribution paid by individuals not otherwise required to contribute who wish to enhance their entitlement to benefit.
- Class 4 – earnings-related contribution payable by those in self-employment and collected with their Schedule D income tax liabilities (see 1.2.4).

The rates in force for 1987/88 can be found in Appendix C.

Primary and secondary Class 1 contributions must be paid in respect of each employment and regardless of whether the payer is also self-employed and liable for Class 2 and Class 4 contributions. However, where contributions are paid in excess of the maximum of either Class 1 contributions or the aggregate of Class 2 and Class 4 contributions in any year, the excess is refunded. An employed earner may apply for deferment of liability for his primary Class 1 contributions in respect of one or more of his employments; or he can make arrangements to pay the maximum in advance, thereby simplifying the mechanics of settling the amount finally due. Application may also be made for a certificate of exemption or deferment in respect of Class 4 contributions where it is likely that no, or a reduced, liability will arise. An application for the deferment or exemption from the payment of Class 2 contributions can also be made for the above reasons or where it is thought that yearly earnings will not exceed certain limits, i.e. £2,125 for 1987/88.

2   The Married Man

2.1   INTRODUCTION

Generally in the UK a husband and wife are taxed as one person with the wife's income and capital gains being treated for tax purposes as those of her husband where they are living together and the husband being responsible for the payment of any taxes arising on his wife's income or gains. Therefore there is a general requirement that all the income of the wife living with her husband must be included in returns of income made by him except where:

(a)   one spouse is resident abroad (see below), *or*
(b)   an election for separate assessment is made (see 2.4).

A married woman is treated for tax purposes as living with her husband unless they are:

(i)   separated under the terms of a court order or by a deed of separation, or
(ii)   they are in fact separated in such circumstances that the separation is likely to be permanent.

However, where a married woman is living with her husband and one of them is and one of them is not resident in the UK for a particular tax year then for that year they are treated as if they were permanently separated, unless it is to their disadvantage so to do.

The husband is therefore liable to pay income tax which is calculated by taking into account joint incomes except:

(a) Where there is an election in force for the separate taxation of the wife's earnings (see 2.3) or for separate assessment (see 2.4).

(b) Where the husband has not paid the tax within 28 days of the due date of payment an assessment can be made on the wife and tax collected from her but the amount recoverable from her cannot exceed her share having regard to her income and gains.

(c) A husband can disclaim liability for tax on his deceased wife's income or gains arising while they were living together by giving notice to her executors and the Revenue within two months after the date of the grant of probate or letters of administration. The deceased wife's executors or administrators have power to extend this time limit. In this situation the Revenue must then collect the tax calculated to be the wife's share using the separate assessment procedure of apportionment (see 2.4) direct from the wife's estate.

(d) Where the husband is unaware of income that his wife has received an Inspector of Taxes may, by concession, make confidential arrangements with her to settle the outstanding tax liability but as one of the conditions of this arrangement she must ensure that for the future her husband is aware of her income.

With certain exceptions, repayments of tax overpaid under the PAYE system are made direct to the wife and the Inspector will notify the husband that this has been done.

2.2   YEAR OF MARRIAGE

In the year of marriage a husband is entitled to receive the higher personal allowance but this is reduced for each complete month from 6 April to the date of the marriage by 1/12th of the difference between this allowance and the single personal allowance, i.e. £1,370 (£3,795 − £3,425) for 1987/88.

The wife is assessed as a single person in respect of the whole of her income or gains for the year of marriage; consequently, income following the marriage is not aggregated with the husband's for that year. This does not apply where the spouses were married on 6 April.

2.3   SEPARATE TAXATION OF WIFE'S EARNINGS

Except in the year of marriage (see 2.2) a wife who has earned income of her own is entitled to a further personal allowance, known as the wife's earned income allowance (£2,425 for 1987/88). This is currently the same as the single person's allowance except that if the wife's earned income is insufficient to cover this allowance the balance is lost;

thus it cannot be used against any of the husband's income or the wife's investment income.

If the husband's income is insufficient to cover the allowances to which he is entitled, then any excess can be used against the wife's income. Thus unutilized allowances can be passed from husband to wife but not vice versa. The subject of full transferability of personal allowances was considered in a Green Paper published on 18 March 1986 (see 2.6.7).

The principle of aggregation of husband's and wife's joint incomes was substantially breached in 1971 when the concept of the *wife's earnings election* was introduced. This enables the husband and wife to elect jointly that the tax due on the wife's earned income should become her own responsibility and not form part of her husband's income for tax purposes. The following particular points should be noted:

(a) The husband loses the married man's allowance and receives only the single person's allowance.

(b) The wife is in effect left in the same situation as before in that her wife's earned income allowance is replaced by a single person's allowance of at present the same amount, i.e. £2,425 for 1987/88.

(c) Each party is entitled to the full basic rate band up to £17,900 for 1987/88 (with the higher rate bands being applied separately to their incomes above that level).

(d) Any investment income of the wife is not covered by the election but continues to be taxed as part of the husband's total income.

(e) The election must be made jointly by both parties, not earlier than six months before, nor later than 12 months after, the tax year for which it is first to apply. Thereafter it continues in operation until revoked; this must be done by both parties jointly not later than 12 months after the end of the tax year for which the election is not to apply.

The joint earnings of the husband and wife must be substantial to make the claim worthwhile, bearing in mind that the husband will forfeit part of his allowances. The precise level at which a claim is advantageous depends on the individuals' circumstances, but it should certainly be considered where the joint earnings exceed £26,500.

EXAMPLE 1

The earnings of Neil and his wife Katie in the 1987/88 tax year are as follows:

Neil	£28,000
Katie	£11,500

Without a wife's earnings election tax is due as follows:

	Total £	Neil £	Katie £
Salary	39,500	28,000	11,500
Less Allowances:			
Married man's allowance	(3,795)	(3,795)	
Wife's earning income allowance	(2,425)		(2,425)
	£33,280	£24,205	£9,075

Chargeable to tax			
@ 27%	17,900	17,900	
@ 40%	2,500	2,500	
@ 45%	5,000	3,805	1,195
@ 50%	7,880		7,880
	£33,280	£24,205	£9,075
Tax due	£12,023	£7,545	£4,478

With wife's earnings election tax is due as follows:

	Total £	Neil £	Katie £
Salary	39,500	28,000	11,500
Less Single person's allowance	(4,850)	(2,425)	(2,425)
	£34,650	£25,575	£9,075
Chargeable to tax			
@ 27%	26,975	17,900	9,075
@ 40%	2,500	2,500	
@ 45%	5,000	5,000	
@ 50%	175	175	
	£34,650	£25,575	£9,075
Tax due	£10,621	£8,171	£2,450
Overall tax saving	£1,402		

2.4   SEPARATE ASSESSMENT

Quite distinct from the wife's earnings election in 2.3 is the election for the separate assessment of wife's income, which provides a formal machinery for a division of the overall liability of husband and wife between them pro rata to their respective income, but does not result in any reduction overall in that ultimate tax liability.

It is, however, possible for both the wife's earnings election and a separate taxation election to be in operation at the same time. Provided the former election is appropriate, this will result in both a reduction in the ultimate tax liability and an apportionment of that liability between husband and wife.

To be effective an application may be made by either spouse within six months before 6 July in any year of assessment in which the wife's income would be aggregated with the husband's. The separate assessment election will continue for subsequent years until notice is given to terminate it, which should be made within six months before 6 July in the year of assessment in which it is no longer required.

Each spouse will now complete and submit separate tax returns to the Inspector of Taxes and be responsible for his/her share of the final tax liability. Where a repayment of income is due in respect of a particular source of income that repayment is made direct to the spouse whose income it is. However, in calculating each spouse's tax liability the total allowances that must be allocated to the wife cannot be less, in terms of tax, than those which she would have been entitled to because she has earned income. If she is unable to use all of the allowances available to her to cover her own tax liability any excess goes to the benefit of the husband and vice versa.

2.5 DEATH

When a marriage ends by the death of one of the spouses the effects are as follows:

(a) The surviving husband remains entitled to the married man's allowance for the whole year. Should he remarry in the year there is no restriction placed on the allowance as described at 2.2 above.

(b) The income of the wife remains that of the husband up to the date of death. Where the wife is the survivor she is treated as a 'feme sole' thereafter and entitled to her own full single personal allowance to be set against her income from the end of the marriage to the following 5 April. She is also entitled to a *widow's bereavement allowance* for the year of her husband's death and for the following year. The widow's bereavement allowance for 1987/88 is £1,370. However, this allowance is forfeited for the following year if the widow remarries before the beginning of that year. This allowance is not available for widowers.

A husband can disclaim liability for tax arising on his deceased wife's income or gains while they were living together by giving notice to her executors and the Revenue within two months after the date of the grant of probate or letters of administration. The deceased wife's executors or administrators have power to extend this time limit. In this situation the Revenue must then collect the tax calculated to be the wife's share using the separate assessment procedure (see 2.4) direct from the wife's estate.

2.6   TAX DISADVANTAGES AND POSSIBLE REFORMS

Overall it is considered that our present tax system penalizes marriage. The main disadvantages are identified below.

2.6.1   Mortgage interest

Two single people are each entitled to tax relief on the interest they pay on up to £30,000 of loans used to buy or improve their main home (see 1.4.2). This amounts to £60,000 in total. However, a married couple living together can get tax relief on loans on a single house up to £30,000.

2.6.2   Capital gains tax

An individual can make net taxable gains of £6,600 in the 1987/88 tax year without incurring any liability to capital gains tax. However, a married couple are entitled to make only £6,600 of gains between them without incurring a tax charge.

Where a husband makes chargeable gains and a wife has allowable losses in a tax year, or vice versa, these are normally netted off against each other in arriving at the net gains or losses for the year. However, either spouse may elect not to have his or her losses taken up in this way but carried forward for relief in a later year; such an election must be made by 5 July following the end of the tax year for which it is to apply.

It is also possible for husband and wife to be *separately assessed* for CGT purposes as they can for income tax (see 2.4). Again, this merely provides a means of apportioning the overall liability between them and does not result in any saving of tax. The election must be made (by either spouse) not later than 5 July following the end of the tax year concerned and then continues until revoked.

2.6.3 Deeds of covenant

Except in the year of marriage (see 2.2), a married couple cannot use covenants in favour of each other to save any tax. Where the couple is unmarried a deed of covenant can be used to utilize personal allowances (see 1.4.3).

2.6.4 Children

A single parent can obtain the additional personal allowance of £1,370 for 1987/88 in addition to the normal single personal allowance of £2,425. This effectively means that a single person is entitled to the equivalent of a married man's allowance, i.e. £3,795. Where two single parents are living together with two children it should be possible for them to receive twice the personal allowances available to a married couple with two children where only the husband works. See also 9.2.2 regarding the position following separation or divorce.

2.6.5 Business expansion scheme

Provided all the qualifying conditions are met business expansion scheme relief should be available where one individual living with another, but not married, invests (up to £40,000) in the other's business, as they are not treated as connected persons for this purpose.

2.6.6 Inheritance tax

The exemption for transfers of capital between spouses (see 1.6.2) does not apply to unmarried couples living together – although a timely marriage just before the death of one of the parties could cure this problem!

2.6.7 Possible reforms

The Government's Green Paper on the reform of personal taxation was published on 18 March 1986. Mr Lawson, the Chancellor of the Exchequer, said that it tackled two main issues. First it contained proposals for reforming 'the structure of personal allowances in general and the treatment of married women in particular, aimed at securing complete equality for men and women'. Secondly it provided proposals for a new structure of personal tax allowances which it was intended would 'take more people out of the poverty and unemployment traps than is possible under the present system for the same cost'.

The Green Paper recognized the tax penalties on marriage and looked for ways of mitigating these and providing help where it is most needed, typically married couples with the responsibilities of caring for a young family or for elderly relatives at home where the wife is least able to take paid work.

It is suggested that a system of transferable allowances would at least partially remedy these defects. The legislation under which a married woman's income is regarded for tax purposes as that of her husband would come to an end, and there would be complete equality of the treatment for men and women for tax purposes. This would apply to savings income as well as to earned income, thus giving women the opportunity for privacy in their tax affairs. It is intended that the various tax penalties on marriage that are a feature of the present tax system would disappear, but the new system would continue to recognize the sharing of responsibilities within a marriage.

It is also intended that the reform would complement the social security system although it is accepted that any major structural reform of income tax is bound to alter the relative burden of tax between different taxpayers or between different stages in the life of the same taxpayer. It seems most likely that the Government would want to implement any reforms in such a way that no couple would suffer a reduction in cash terms in their total allowances during the period of change.

The Green Paper also discusses a number of other possible long-term options including:

(a) Streamlining the relationship between the tax and social security systems.

(b)   The possibility of amalgamating employees' national insurance contributions with income tax.

(c)   Changes to the administration of income tax which should be made possible by computerization.

(d)   Some specific matters such as the abolition of certain allowances if transferable allowances are introduced and changing the way in which interest relief is given on the first £30,000 of loan moneys used to acquire a main residence. A change being considered is to relate the loan limit to the residence itself rather than to each individual or married couple thereby lifting this particular penalty on marriage.

As any structural changes in the tax system will have to wait on completion of the Revenue's massive computerization programme, it is unlikely that anything major in this area will be implemented before 1992 at the earliest.

3 Children

3.1 TAX POSITION AS PART OF THE FAMILY UNIT

A child is usually treated as a separate individual for tax purposes with all his income being assessable on him but with full entitlement to personal allowances and reliefs. The most valuable personal relief that all children should strive to use by whatever means necessary is the personal allowance, which for 1987/88 is £2,425. If income of this amount were received which was all taxed at source a tax repayment of £654·75 (£2,425 at 27%) would be released.

The exception to the general rule above is where a parent creates a settlement in favour of his own child. In this situation the income is treated as that of the parent while the child is under 18 years of age and remains unmarried. This position covers all situations where the parent is the source of the capital which produces the income and will also extend to settlements created where the income is, or may become, payable to or for the benefit of a child of the parent settlor. There are some exceptions to these rules as follows:

(a)   where the aggregate amount of the income paid to or for the benefit of the child in any one tax year does not exceed £5;

(b)   where the parent is not chargeable to income tax because he or she is not resident in the United Kingdom;

(c)   accumulation settlements where all the capital and income of the settlement is accumulated and none is paid to, or for the benefit of, the child (see 3.4). (Note that this does not need to be as restricted in its terms as the 'accumulation and maintenance settlement' described in 1.6.5.)

For the above purposes, the child 'includes a stepchild, an adopted child, and an illegitimate child' and 'stepchild' includes a child of the wife by a previous marriage.

In short, any provision made by a parent for the benefit of his child may create a settlement whether there is a requirement to do so or merely a parental obligation. On the other hand, the Revenue does not treat payments made under a court order as being under a settlement for these purposes.

3.2   DEEDS OF COVENANT

3.2.1   Parents

As explained in 1.4.3, by executing deeds of covenant rather than making voluntary payments to non-taxpayers it may be possible to utilize personal reliefs or exemptions against the gross equivalent of payments made. Thus covenants may be executed by parents in favour of their adult children who are over 18 years of age or who are married. An effective covenant cannot be made by a parent in favour of an unmarried child under 18 years of age.

This is a particularly attractive arrangement where the child is still undergoing full-time education and, because of the parents' income, is receiving no or a reduced grant so that it is expected that the parents will contribute to the maintenance of their offspring. The most tax-efficient way of meeting any shortfall is by way of a deed of covenant so that most, if not all, of the child's personal allowances can be utilized thereby releasing a tax repayment. The Revenue has effectively endorsed this tax saving arrangement by producing a pack (IR59) which includes a pro-forma deed of covenant to be executed by the parent in these situations.

This type of deed must be capable of exceeding six years. However, it is not essential that the deed itself lasts at least seven years, merely that it must be *capable* of doing so. Therefore, it should be in order to provide for the deed to expire on the earlier of the seventh anniversary or the cessation of full-time education.

The execution of such deeds, while proving tax efficient, may have unforeseen consequences as regards grants awarded by local authorities and social security benefits receivable by the student during holiday periods. Generally, the grant-awarding authority does not take into account income received from covenants executed by parents when assessing the student's resources and the level of educational grant appropriate. Consequently the parent is unable to claim the covenanted payment as a deduction for the purposes of the related means test.

However, such income will be taken into account for social security purposes where the payment is on an annual basis. In effect the covenanted payment will be divided by 52 and this will represent a student's income in any particular week. This may restrict entitlement to social security benefits. The government has announced that with effect from 2 December 1985, where there is a parental contribution to the grant and that contribution is paid under a deed of covenant, the student will suffer no reduction of benefit entitlement. Where no grant is paid, the parental contribution is regarded as equal to the maximum ordinary maintenance grant for the student's course. Where a parent chooses to provide income in excess of this amount the excess will be taken into account in reducing benefit in the normal way over a full year but excluding the first £4 per week. This whole matter is still under review.

However, there is a school of thought that it would be in order for payments to be made by reference to the term periods so that during the vacations no income is receivable by the student and consequently a full claim for benefit may be made.

3.2.2 Grandparents and other relatives

Although, as mentioned above, it is not possible for a parent to make an effective covenant in favour of his unmarried minor child, it is possible for covenants to be executed by grandparents, uncles, aunts, godparents, friends, etc. which can be tax effective provided that there is no element of *reciprocity*. Reciprocity extends from a simple arrangement involving two groups of parents executing covenants in favour of each other's offspring to complex arrangements involving any number of groups of parents executing deeds for the next child(ren) in the chain.

One difficulty that may arise concerning reciprocity is where a grandparent contracts to pay school fees direct to a school for the benefit of a child and later executes a deed of covenant which is intended to meet the cost of providing schooling. It can be said that there is reciprocity in this respect as a grandparent has cancelled his or her direct liability to pay school fees by executing the deed.

Another practice that the Revenue is aware of is where a deed of covenant is executed but no actual payments have been made – the only reason the deed was created was to obtain the tax repayment. To counter this arrangement it is becoming quite common for the Revenue to ask for evidence that the payment has been made, perhaps by seeing bank statements supporting the transfer of funds.

As in 3.2.1 such deeds must be capable of exceeding six years. Here again, it may be appropriate to retain the option to terminate them on the cessation of full-time education if this could occur earlier than the expiry of seven years.

Where there are a number of grandchildren it may be more convenient for a grandparent to make one covenant to a trustee of a discretionary settlement who has powers to distribute the money among the beneficiaries as he or she considers appropriate. This approach is obviously more flexible and can allow for changes in circumstances. The discretionary beneficiaries are in the same position overall as if the amount paid to them had been paid direct under a separate deed. Where covenanted income remains undistributed it is treated as continuing to be income of the covenantor for all tax purposes.

3.3 PLANNING FOR SCHOOL FEES

3.3.1 Introduction

The commitment to pay the cost of educating children privately is likely to be a family's largest financial commitment next to buying a house. However, with the continuing experience of disruption in the public sector it appears that more and more people are willing to shoulder the financial burdens necessary in order that their children can be educated with as few distractions as possible. To a great extent this is an all-or-nothing commitment. Once the child has attended a fee-paying school and experienced this style of education it may be difficult for him to make the change should it become necessary to revert to state education.

As a basic principle it is important to retain a degree of flexibility in whatever arrangements are made to allow for changed circumstances in relation to the family, the choice of school and even government policy.

School fees can be paid directly out of capital or income

as and when they fall due but there are a number of methods that may be considered more appropriate:

(a) school fees composition scheme (see 3.3.2);
(b) educational trust (see 3.3.3);
(c) fixed interest scheme (see 3.3.4);
(d) scheme using a temporary annuity (see 3.3.5);
(e) life assurance based scheme (see 3.3.6);
(f) unit trust regular savings scheme (see 3.3.7).

3.3.2 School fees composition scheme

Under this type of arrangement a lump sum is paid in advance to the chosen school. This will be less than the total fees that it is meant to fund to reflect the discount offered by the school because it has the use of the money prior to it being needed to educate the child. The actual size of discount offered by the school will depend upon the time lapse between the date of payment and the date the child's education is to commence at school and the level of interest rates prevailing at the time the lump sum payment is made. This approach could be attractive to a higher rate taxpayer where the school has educational charity status, as no income tax or capital gains tax liabilities can arise on him from the investment of the lump sum by the school.

This is a simple and convenient scheme but is not without its difficulties. A problem may occur where the child does not attend that particular school or if he should die. In these circumstances the lump sum may be returned but usually with a poor rate of interest.

3.3.3   Educational trust

This is effectively an independent version of the school fees composition scheme mentioned above. The difference is that the trustees pay the school fees for the child concerned. This means that it is not necessary to make a final decision on which school is appropriate until shortly before the first payment becomes due.

Where circumstances change it should also be possible to switch funds for the benefit of other children in the family if necessary. Where the child dies before all the capital has been utilized the balance should be repaid together with some interest.

3.3.4   Fixed interest scheme

Here capital can be planned to be available at particular points in the future and is not specifically linked to the provision of school fees; i.e. as the capital is realized it can be used for any purpose.

Under this type of arrangement typically a number of suitable fixed interest investments are acquired, perhaps gilt-edged securities or National Savings Certificates, which at the time they reach maturity are timed to coincide with the payment of a tranche of school fees. This approach is very flexible when the funds are realized but some planning and early action are needed to ensure that maturity dates coincide, within reason, with the times that the funds are required. There may also be a measure of administrative work necessary in making sure that relatively small amounts of income are reinvested and that that income is declared for tax purposes.

3.3.5 Scheme using a temporary annuity

In this situation capital is used to purchase a temporary annuity the income from which can be used to pay the school fees.

3.3.6 Life assurance based scheme

There are a number of different types of qualifying life assurance policies available on the market from which the proceeds can be received completely tax free provided certain conditions are met. Therefore, where it is possible to commence paying premium payments for a minimum period of ten years before the time when school fees are required, the following policies may be suitable:

(a) A series of endowment with profits policies which will mature in successive years coinciding with the beginning of term time. One advantage is that a competitive return, particularly for higher rate tax-payers, is usually obtained and matters can be arranged so that maturity proceeds increase each year in order to cover, at least in part, any increase in education costs due to inflation, etc.

(b) Flexible endowment policies which will allow the policyholder to decide when the proceeds should be received. These usually cost more to administer.

(c) Unit linked policies that use the tax-free income facility which is available after the policy has been held for ten years. As the value of such policies depends upon the underlying investment the ultimate proceeds can fluctuate and it is therefore usually advisable to link any such policy to a stable rather than a volatile fund.

As with the fixed interest scheme (see 3.3.4) one of the advantages of using life policies is that they are very flexible as the proceeds on maturity can be applied for any other purpose if required.

3.3.7   Unit trust regular savings scheme

A number of unit trusts operate regular savings plans, usually on a monthly basis. These plans are quite flexible and it is possible to terminate them at any time without penalty. Over the longer term, obviously dependent upon the investment markets, it is possible that they may produce more value than a life assurance policy, but the return is not guaranteed. This type of investment may be best in a stable of investments that may eventually be used to pay school fees.

3.3.8   Funding from other sources

There are a number of other ways in which funds could be organized to provide for school fees. These might include gifts from grandparents or relatives, perhaps by using deeds of covenant or setting up an accumulation and maintenance settlement or possibly a discretionary trust (see 1.6.5).

3.4 BARE TRUSTEE SETTLEMENTS

Notwithstanding the anti-avoidance provisions mentioned in 3.1 it is possible for a parent to transfer a sum of money to a deposit account in the name of bare trustees for the absolute benefit of the child. Provided the income accumulates and is not paid to the child until the age of 18, the income will be treated as the child's. No tax liability arises as long as the child's income does not exceed the personal allowance for the year, although the income must be entered on the child's income tax return.

4 Planning for Retirement and Old Age

4.1 INTRODUCTION

Present government policy is to give greater encouragement to individuals organizing their own pension provision rather than relying on the state. The opportunities for investing for one's future in this way are great, as are the powers to control the moneys invested.

4.2 STATE BENEFITS

The basic element in almost everyone's retirement income is the flat-rate basic state retirement pension. This is payable provided that national insurance contributions have been paid for the greater part of the individual's working life based on a sliding scale.

A woman entitled to a pension in her own right will normally receive it at the age of 60, a man at the age of 65. A married man will receive an additional amount for his wife but if she is entitled to pensions in respect of both her own and her husband's contributions, she may claim whichever is the higher pension.

In addition to paying national insurance contributions it is also possible to pay into a pension scheme. It is the role of the state to make sure that schemes run privately by employers meet certain standards and in cases where the pensions granted by such schemes have their value eroded by inflation, the state supplements the pension payable.

There is a national earnings-related pension scheme run by the state, and since 1978 every employer has had to pay into the state scheme for all his employees unless he is running an approved private scheme. Along with many other aspects of the social security system this is under active review by the government and a Green Paper on its workings was recently published.

For the position of British nationals living or working overseas see Chapter 7.

The state scheme offers a considerable improvement on the terms of pension schemes that were being run before 1978. All the benefits increase in line with the increases in the retail prices index, but there are still a number of disadvantages that the state scheme has when compared with a private occupational scheme that has been duly approved. There can be no flexibility on the age of retirement. There is no income tax relief for the individual's payments into the scheme, and at the present time (1987/88) earnings over £15,340 are unpensionable.

4.3 OCCUPATIONAL PENSION SCHEMES

4.3.1 Introduction

The provision of a good pension scheme is a very tax-efficient way of supplementing the state retirement pension and likely to be a significant ingredient of any employee's remuneration package. Subject to formal approval by the Superannuation Funds Office of the Inland Revenue such schemes will normally have the following features:

(a) Employees' contributions are deductible for tax purposes but not for national insurance contribution purposes.

(b) Employers' contributions are deductible for tax purposes and not treated as a taxable benefit in the hands of employees.

(c) The fund is exempt from income tax on investment income and capital gains tax on normal investment transactions although it is subject to stamp duty, petroleum revenue tax and VAT.

(d) A maximum pension (taxable under Schedule E) limited to 2/3rds final salary (see 4.3.2) after a minimum of 20 years' service with a reduction for shorter periods of pensionable service.

(e) There is usually a facility to commute part of the pension payable at retirement for a tax-free lump sum up to 1½ times final salary after a minimum of 20 years' service; for pension schemes set up after 17

March 1987 and for individuals entering an existing scheme after that date, this will be subject to an overriding limit of £150,000.

(f) A widow(er)'s pension up to 2/3rds of the employee's pension plus dependant's benefits, i.e. a maximum widow(er)'s pension of 4/9ths of final remuneration as a 'commencement' level but the total of widow(er)'s and/or dependant's pensions cannot exceed the member's own entitlement.

(g) Death-in-service benefits:

    (i) A tax-free lump sum of up to four times salary at the time of death in addition to the return of the employee's contributions plus reasonable interest. From a tax planning point of view it may be appropriate to have such a benefit effectively written in trust so that it does not fall to be taken into the estate of the deceased for inheritance tax but may be distributed by the trustees of the pension scheme using their discretion direct to nominated beneficiaries (see 5.3.2).

    (ii) A widow(er)'s pension up to 2/3rds of the member's pension entitlement assuming that he or she had reached normal retirement age at the date of his or her death.

(h) The fund may increase payments after retirement to make some allowance for inflation.

Where a scheme is established it can be either contracted in or contracted out of the state scheme. Where the scheme is contracted out the employer undertakes to provide the benefits the state would otherwise have provided and in return both the employee and the employer pay reduced rates of Class 1 national insurance contributions. The government is currently reviewing the sphere of social security spending and it seems likely that some changes will be made to this arrangement.

Once money has entered the pension fund it is not available to be specifically used in the business except where the scheme is a self-administered pension scheme as described in 4.7. Also, any benefits payable out of the fund may be related to the employee's salary rather than to the amount of contributions made and consequently an employee who leaves before he would normally retire is likely to be at a disadvantage with a substantial reduction being made in the potential pension benefits available.

The only restriction on the level of investment that the employer may make in such a fund is the overall funding requirement of the scheme, i.e. there must be sufficient capital available to meet the obligations likely to be imposed on the fund.

'Controlling' directors (i.e. those with 5% or more of the share capital) may participate in occupational pension schemes of companies.

As the contracting-in or -out rules did not take effect until 1978, employers are not required to give credit for service before that date. In practice, however, most contracted-out employers had occupational schemes before 1978 and so will pay pensions in respect of service before these rules came into effect.

Partly due to the complexity of the legislation and partly due to the fact that the requirements of various employees and employers are so different, each scheme is essentially tailor-made to suit particular needs. In practice, this entails liaison between the company, representatives of the employees, accountants, solicitors and insurance brokers in devising a suitable scheme.

4.3.2 Definition of 'final salary'

This is defined as either

(a) any of the previous five years' emoluments; or

(b) the average of the best three or more consecutive years' emoluments ending not more than ten years prior to retirement. This definition is obligatory for '20% directors', i.e. those who control directly or indirectly more than 20% of the voting shares. In determining what is final remuneration years 1, 2 and 3 before retirement, or indeed years 9, 10 and 11, can be chosen for review. All years chosen except the last year before retirement can be indexed using the retail prices index to produce a revalued set of figures.

For schemes set up on or after 17 March 1987 and for individuals joining an existing scheme on or after that date, in calculating the amount of lump-sum payment that may be taken as in 4.3.1.(e) above, emoluments are generally limited to £100,000. It follows therefore that normally the maximum lump sum that may be taken in these circumstances is £150,000.

Certain provisions were included in the second 1987 Finance Act to prevent 'abuse' of this definition, for example by boosting the final year's earnings.

4.3.3   Guaranteed minimum pension

Employers are not obliged to increase pensions once they are in payment. This is why the state provides supplementary bonuses to partially protect contracted-out pensions from inflation (see 4.2). The state bonuses are linked to that part of a person's pension which he would have received if he had been in the state earnings-related scheme instead. This is called the 'guaranteed minimum pension'. The state inflation proofing is provided in addition to any increase paid by the employer. Some employers provide almost full inflation proofing for their employees' pensions; others provide occasional rises which only partly compensate for inflation.

4.4   PENSION RIGHTS WHEN CHANGING JOBS

An employee who moves from one employer to another may lose part of his pension rights. He may have a choice of:

(a)   Accepting a deferred pension, usually payable from normal retirement date with a post-retirement widow-(er)'s pension. A deferred or 'frozen' pension is a pension preserved by the former employer and normally linked to the employee's pay at the date the employment ceased. In its basic form this provides no protection against inflation. If pay levels rise before retirement a pension linked to a salary from some years before will look very small when it is paid. Deferred benefits must be available once five years' qualifying service has been completed.

Deferred benefits can be increased before or after they commence to be paid at a rate determined, either fixed or variable, at the discretion of the trustees of the fund. However benefits accruing from service after January 1985 must be revalued each year in line with the retail prices index but subject to a maximum increase of 5% per annum compound.

The maximum permitted by the Revenue is the greater of 1/60th of final remuneration for each year of actual service with a maximum of 40 years or, if it is more favourable, the amount calculated by the following formula:

$$2/3\text{rds final salary} \times \frac{\text{service completed}}{\text{total potential years of service}}$$

Where the scheme is contracted out, due to the state earnings-related provisions, at least part of an employee's entitlement must be inflation proofed under the guaranteed minimum pension (GMP) arrangements. This is related to the benefits that would have been provided had the member been contracted into the state scheme.

The GMP must be revalued, using the retail prices index, up to the State pension age, 65 years for men and 60 for women, and this can increase substantially the amount of deferred pension that has to be provided. However, the state earnings-related pension entitlement is reduced by the amount of the revalued GMP payable resulting in no overall effect as far as the member is concerned but imposing a greater burden on the scheme whilst relieving the state.

(b) Accepting an early retirement pension calculated according to the particular pension scheme's rules. The pension may be based on final remuneration at the time of leaving; thus account may be taken of any cost-of-living increases between that time and normal retirement date, but on the other hand it may not. This option is usually available only where the employee is at least 50 years of age, although a female employee may retire with immediate benefits before age 50 (but not before age 45) if her normal retirement age is lower than 60 and she is already within ten years of it. This point may be reviewed in the light of a recent decision of the European Court concerning sex discrimination.

The maximum immediate pension is the greater of 1/60th of final remuneration for each year of actual service with a maximum of 40 years or, if it is more favourable, the amount calculated by the formula given in (a).

The widow(er)'s pension could be two-thirds of this amount. Individual pension schemes may have arrangements to discount the pension payable by a percentage varying with time to take into account advance payment.

(c) Transferring his pension rights to his new employer.

Transfer payments are almost universally accepted by pension schemes. Some use the receipts to back-date the effective commencement date of the employment for pension purposes, while others, in particular insured schemes, make a fixed addition to the pension ultimately payable.

The advantage in obtaining added years is that the final benefit is an increased percentage of final salary and this method can therefore be expected to provide a measure of inflation proofing. Normally a transfer payment would represent the whole of an employee's benefits from the transferring scheme, but the Super-annuation Funds Office does not object to partial transfer payments, coupled with retention in the first scheme of certain residual benefits such as for widows and dependants.

(d) Extinguishing part or all of his pension rights in return for a refund of some or all of his own contributions.

Refunds will usually be available only for contributions made before April 1975 or for short periods of pensionable service up to five years. From 1988 this period is to be reduced to two years.

As a general point it is not usually wise to take a refund in respect of periods of service up to 5 April 1975 (with a deferred pension for the remaining period) as the benefits forgone may be worth more than the refund obtained. Where a refund is taken, any benefit that would be derived from the employer's contributions is lost.

When an individual decides to take the lump sum option and the pension scheme is contracted out of the state scheme there is a requirement on the trustees prior to releasing funds to the member to buy him back into the state scheme. Tax at the rate of 10% is deducted from the amount payable to the employee.

(e) Opting for a Section 32 pension buy-out annuity. In this situation the transfer value that would usually be available to be transferred to a new pension scheme under the arrangements described at (c) above is used to purchase an individual deferred annuity from an insurance company held in the name of the member. The leaver thereby receives the benefit of the whole amount of his own and the employer's contributions. On reaching retirement age the individual can take an 'open market option' to buy the best annuity available in the market at that particular time, subject to the overriding general limit on the amount of pension that can be paid.

Various types of policy are available from insurance companies including non-profit or with-profit deferred annuities, unit linked contracts and deposit administration policies. Part of the available funds would of necessity be invested in a non-profit (guaranteed) fund in order to protect the GMP benefit that had accrued.

From 1 January 1986 early leavers have the option to purchase such an annuity as of right. Also, the legislation overrides the rules of pension schemes, making it mandatory for them to offer this alternative.

Where, as part of a termination agreement (see Chapter 8), the employer makes a special contribution to an approved scheme to provide benefits for the employee, the Revenue has stated that it will not seek to charge such a payment under the provisions taxing lump sum payments. This is provided the benefits on retirement are within the limits and in the form prescribed by the rules of the scheme.

The Government has expressed concern about the problems of transferability of pension rights and is having consultations with insurance companies and other pension providers with a view to bringing in regulations to allow complete freedom of transfer rights.

4.5 ADDITIONAL VOLUNTARY CONTRIBUTIONS

Those who would not expect to obtain maximum benefits under the scheme and particularly those nearing retirement should consider paying the largest contributions possible so as to secure as near the maximum benefits as they can.

An employee is able to contribute up to a maximum of 15% of his total remuneration in addition to any contributions that the employer makes. In most cases, members of approved occupational pension schemes are required to contribute much less than 15% and it may therefore be possible for the employee to make up all or part of the difference by paying *additional voluntary contributions* ('AVCs') either connected with the main pension scheme or into a separate plan. For maximum flexibility a separate plan may be preferable as the contributor is usually able to see precisely how his own investments are faring and his contributions can be segregated from the moneys held in the main pension fund.

An alternative is for the employee to enter into a salary sacrifice arrangement. Under these arrangements the employee requests that remuneration to which he does not have any contractual entitlement, such as a discretionary bonus, is invested by the company in a separate pension scheme; this may also be arranged in relation to remuneration contractually due provided that the amount required is waived before entitlement actually arises. One drawback here is that any future pension entitlement from the main scheme may be based on 'final salary' which has thereby been reduced. However, subject to the terms of the scheme on what constitutes 'final salary', this problem may be circumvented by this arrangement being dispensed with in the final years of the employment.

Previously, contributions to an AVC scheme had to be made on a regular basis and be paid for at least five years or to normal retirement date if earlier. The Superannuation Funds Office may, however, allow the contributions to be discontinued earlier if changed circumstances mean that the payments are causing hardship.

However, much greater freedom will be allowed in the payment of AVCs with effect from October 1987. This will allow an employee to pay additional contributions (referred to as 'free standing' contributions) into an entirely separate plan, not tied to his employer's scheme, without any prior commitment as to amount or timing; in particular the five-year requirement has been dropped.

There will be certain constraints to these arrangements:

(1) The benefits generated by the additional contributions must not lead to the overall level of benefit exceeding that normally approved by the Revenue (see 4.3.1).

(2) It will not now be possible for the employee to commute any part of the additional pension rights generated by the contributions for a capital sum (as in paragraph (e) of 4.3.1), and he will normally be required to draw the full amount of the extra pension.

4.6 SELF-EMPLOYED RETIREMENT ANNUITIES

For those individuals who are self-employed or in non-pensionable employment where there is no occupational pension scheme available, separate arrangements may be made using retirement annuity contracts. These are equivalent to 'money purchase' schemes where a sum of money is invested in a fund where it can grow tax free and ultimately the funds available are used to acquire the best annuity possible in the market at that time.

The benefits possible under these arrangements as opposed to those available under occupational pension schemes are restricted in two ways. The first restriction is the amount of the maximum premiums which are permitted to be paid into these types of policies. These are related to a percentage of 'net relevant earnings' and the age of the person concerned at the time of the payment. Net relevant earnings are profits or earnings from the business or non-pensionable employment after certain deductions such as expenses, trading losses and capital allowances.

Up to 5 April 1987, the maximum percentages of net relevant earnings were as shown below:

Year of birth	Percentage of net relevant earnings
1934 or any later year	17·5
1916–1933	20·0
1914 or 1915	21·0
1912 or 1913	24·0

With effect from 6 April 1987, the percentage is now governed by the employee's age, as follows:

Age	Percentage of net relevant earnings
Up to 50	17·5
51–55	20·0
56–60	22·5
61–75	27·5

The other restriction is that by the very nature of these schemes all the contributions paid by a policyholder go into building up a cash fund which must ultimately finance the contributor's pension. There is no question of his ultimate pension being related explicitly to profits or earnings in the years leading up to retirement. When normal retirement date is reached, as most policies have an open market option, the policyholder can go into the market and buy the best annuity possible at that time from whichever company is offering the best rates. However, interest rates dictate the pension payable and as they are prone to fairly major fluctuations timing can be critical.

The main benefits that can be enjoyed are as follows:

(a) A retirement pension – this can commence at the minimum age of 60 (50 for contracts taken out on or after 4 January 1988) although for persons in certain occupations they may commence earlier. The pension must, in any event, be taken not later than age 75.

(b) Instead of a full pension, for contracts taken out on or after 4 January 1988 a tax-free lump sum can be taken at retirement of up to 25% of the accumulated fund.

For contracts taken out prior to 4 January 1988 the limits are differently calculated as follows:

Date of contract	*Normal maximum*	*Overriding maximum*
Prior to 17 March 1987	Three times remaining pension after taking lump sum	Not applicable
Between 18 March 1987 and 3 January 1988 (both dates inclusive)	As above	£150,000 per contract

(c) On death before retirement a lump sum can be provided for a widow or dependants by allocating up to 5% of net relevant earnings (as defined earlier) to a separate scheme. This has to come out of the maximum allowable contributions of 17½% of net relevant earnings (or higher) as set out above.

(d) For a lower pension commencing at normal retirement date an element of increase in future pension receipts can be allowed for.

(e) Should the contributor die before reaching normal retirement age contributions paid will normally be returned, possibly with interest. However, the amount recoverable cannot exceed the total value of the pension fund at the time of death.

Tax relief is given on contributions at the individual's highest income tax rate. Premiums paid in a particular tax year can be offset against income in that year or related back to the previous year of assessment. Should there be no profits or earnings in that year the premium can be related back a further 12-month period. The claim for this treatment has to be sent to the Revenue by 5 July following the year of assessment in which the premium is paid. It is also possible to make retrospective premium payments so that for each of the tax years up to seven years before the year in which the premium is paid the maximum relief possible, depending on profits arising in those years, can be utilized.

4.7 SELF-ADMINISTERED SCHEMES

These are essentially approved occupational pension schemes with a difference. There will generally be less than 12 members and those members may also be trustees, thereby controlling the investment of their own pension moneys. Such schemes are very flexible and, while their primary aim is to secure pension benefits for their members, they can contribute to the success of the main business. For instance, up to 50% of the pension fund can be lent, on commercial terms, to the employer and the fund may also invest in property which may be leased to the company at a commercial rent. Benefits for members can be arranged to suit particular individual needs and it is possible to vary the level and timing of contributions.

These schemes can be very beneficial where the annual contribution is at least £10,000 and where at inception employees are not likely to retire in the near future. However, significant costs may be incurred in setting up the scheme and in necessary administration. The investment abilities and performance of the trustees will ultimately be reflected in the level of benefits ultimately receivable by the member.

Before giving approval to such a scheme, the Superannuation Funds Office will require that one of the trustees of the fund is a pensioneer trustee. This has to be an individual or body, independent of the employer, well experienced in the field of occupational schemes. The pensioneer trustee is required to give certain undertakings as to the winding up of the scheme and as to its management generally.

The Superannuation Funds Office will want to review the progress of the fund on a regular basis, particularly with regard to its investment policy and to transactions between the trustees and the employer company, so as to be satisfied that the fund is being operated in the best interests of the eventual pensioners.

While the concept has many attractions, particularly on the investment side, it does need to be considered with care, particularly to ensure that the interests of all members are adequately protected. It is essential that specialist professional advice, in the legal and taxation field as well as in the pension area itself, be obtained before going into such a scheme.

4.8   LOANBACK ARRANGEMENTS

This is a facility which can be of interest to individuals who are making their own pension provision by way of retirement annuities or for those enhancing their future pension entitlement by paying additional voluntary contributions.

Loans can be obtained from financial institutions which can be related to the provision of a pension or enhanced benefits. A popular arrangement is for an individual to borrow funds from a bank or building society to purchase his main residence with the proceeds, the commutation element from the policy on death or maturity being used to pay the lending institution in discharge of the loan. This provides their support for the funds advanced to purchase the property; as the mortgage is linked to the pension fund, interest need be paid only as in the endowment method of purchasing property on mortgage.

All policies of this type are non-assignable and are

therefore not strictly available to be used as security for a loan. The provider of mortgage funds is merely recognizing the existence of the pension scheme giving an anticipated access to funds that will be available at a future date, and lending up to a certain limit which will represent a multiple of either the annual contribution or a percentage of the tax-free lump sum expected at retirement date.

One important condition that may be imposed upon the borrower is that the loan will become repayable should the pension contributions cease. Care is needed therefore because, if the borrower should suffer ill-health or there is a general decline in his business activity, or should he become unemployed, the lender has the power to demand repayment of the loan immediately; if there are insufficient funds available to meet this demand it may be necessary to sell the property or realize other savings at what may be a difficult time financially.

Any decision by a future Government to tax these lump sums may make this method of borrowing money less sound.

4.9 SICK-PAY AND DISABILITY SCHEMES

Where an employee receives any sums which are paid in connection with his absence from work through sickness or disability, as a result of arrangements entered into by his employer, then the sums will be taxed under Schedule E. Sums paid to a member of the employee's family or household (i.e. spouse, sons and daughters and their spouses, parents and dependants) or to the order or benefit of the employee or his family will be similarly taxed.

Where the scheme is funded by contributions from both employer and employee, only that part of the sick-pay attributable to the employer's contributions will be taxable.

The right of a higher paid employee or director to receive such sums is not classed as a taxable benefit, i.e. the cost to the employer of providing such sick-pay cover will not of itself be taxed as a benefit in kind.

The Inland Revenue concession which previously granted a tax holiday of up to two years on sickness benefits paid under an insurance policy or trust deed has been amended to exclude employer-financed sickness pay schemes and the employer-financed proportion of jointly funded schemes. The concession will continue to apply to benefits paid under schemes entered into and financed by individuals and to the employee's proportion where the scheme is funded jointly.

Payments under the 'statutory sick pay' scheme which came into operation on 6 April 1983 are liable to PAYE and national insurance contributions.

4.10   DEATH-IN-SERVICE AND ACCIDENT POLICIES

An occupational pension scheme may provide for injury cover such as lump sum payments on loss of limbs and/or life cover. In such circumstances, it is normal practice for the Inland Revenue to ignore the taxable benefit arising in respect of a proportion of the contributions and in any case the point is normally settled at the time of negotiation in seeking approval of the scheme. In such cases, it is most important to demonstrate that the benefits arising are discretionary and consequently it is necessary to ensure that the employer first becomes entitled to the benefits under the scheme (the subsequent payment to the employee or his dependants being a separate transaction). If injury and life cover are provided under a separate scheme, any taxable benefit that may arise will be valued under the general rules applicable to *benefits in kind* under income tax Schedule E (see 1.2.5).

Alternatively, an employer may make *voluntary* payments on death or in the event of injury. If a lump sum is paid, it will be tax free, but if a series of recurring payments (i.e. a 'discretionary' pension) is involved, they may be taxed as earned income. The capital sum may be used for purchasing an annuity and the capital element thereof will be free of income tax. A difficult consideration is the question of the deductibility of the payments as regards the employer and particularly so if the recipient has a significant share ownership in the company. If the payments are disallowed and the employer company is close (broadly, one that is under the control of five or fewer shareholders or of its directors), there may be inheritance tax consequences as well.

4.11 'TOP-HAT' SCHEMES

It will be seen from 4.2 above that an employee who is contracted-in to the state scheme and who is not in an occupational pension scheme may have non-pensionable earnings. If this is so, it is possible for the individual employee to make his own pension arrangements with an insurance company in respect of the unpensioned salary. It is also possible to build into such a scheme benefits missing from the state scheme, e.g. tax-free lump sums on retirement or death in service. In these circumstances it is possible to set up a 'one-man' occupational pension scheme for that individual alone. The employer *must* make some contributions to the scheme, though these need not be substantial; the employee may make contributions up to 15% of earnings. Further contributions may be made by the employee taking a corresponding reduction in his salary which the employer pays over. These schemes are referred to as 'top hat' policies.

Alternatively an employee may set up a retirement annuity scheme to which he alone contributes (see 4.6) or, with effect from 4 January 1988, a personal pension scheme (see 4.12).

In addition to this it is also possible to set up a small self-administered scheme (see 4.7) for one person or a small group of people who hold key positions in a small business. This can incorporate loan-back facilities (see 4.8) for the director or employee concerned.

4.12 PERSONAL PENSION SCHEMES

With effect from 4 January 1988, a new and radical concept is to be introduced enabling employees, whether or not they are already in an occupational scheme, to make their own personal pension arrangements.

The new tax regime is to be based on that already described for self-employed retirement annuities in 4.6, and indeed the legislation introduced in the second 1987 Finance Act governs both the new personal pension schemes and interacts with existing schemes. The new arrangements therefore include all the features described in 4.6 with the following additional aspects:

(1) A member of an existing occupational scheme will not normally be allowed to set up a personal pension scheme as well, but he will be able to withdraw from an occupational scheme so as to be free to make his own arrangements if he wishes.

(2) Provided that suitable safeguards are included to preserve his rights under the earnings-related pension element of the state scheme (see 4.2), it will be possible for the employee effectively to contract out of this part of the state scheme, in the same way as may be done with an occupational scheme as described in 4.3.1.

(3) Contributions into an approved personal pension scheme may come from three sources:

(a) the employee;

(b) the employer (if he so wishes);

(c) where the scheme is contracted out as in (1) above, the DHSS will pay over to the scheme managers the difference between the full and contracted-out rates of national insurance contributions (at present amounting to 6·25% of earnings between £39 and £295 per week). Thus there is no reduction in the rates of national insurance contributions actually payable corresponding to that which applies in the case of a contracted out occupational pension scheme.

(4) The total of contributions payable under (3)(a) and (b) (but ignoring any amounts payable under (c)) must not exceed the limits now laid down for self-employed retirement annuity premiums in 4.6, i.e.

Age	Percentage of net relevant earnings
Up to 50	17·5
51–55	20·0
56–60	22·5
61–75	27·5

These contributions may be divided between employer and employee as they agree and there is no requirement for the employer to contribute at all.

(5) Because it will not be possible to take account of individuals' contributions in their PAYE codings on a timely basis, basic rate income tax relief will be given on premiums paid by deduction at source, similar to the MIRAS scheme for mortgage interest relief. Any higher rate relief will be given by assessment.

(6) The employees' proportion of DHSS contributions paid over under (3)(c) above will be 'grossed up' at

the basic rate; this recognizes the fact that the individual has already borne his part of the contribution out of net taxed income, since employees' national insurance contributions do not qualify for tax relief.

Clearly the value of the pension and other benefits that a personal pension scheme can provide will depend on the total contributions that go into it. In this respect the benefits will be less certain than those available under an occupational pension scheme based on 'final salary'.

On the other hand, where an individual has a number of job changes it may be difficult in practice to build up maximum benefits through participation in a succession of occupational schemes and it may be more attractive to make full contributions (possibly with the assistance of employers and the DHSS) into a personal scheme with no transferability problems.

4.13 PURCHASED LIFE ANNUITIES

These are specifically aimed at taxpayers who require an income from capital to be received in a tax-efficient way perhaps guaranteed for a specific period or for the annuitant's lifetime. The investment return will be greater the older the individual is at the time of purchase.

The essential feature of such an annuity is that the future right to income is purchased with a capital sum today which becomes irretrievable. Annuities of this nature can run immediately the capital payment is made or from a prearranged date some time in the future. Annuities may also run for the lifetime of the annuitant, for a predetermined period or for a guaranteed period that may continue after the annuitant's death.

A purchased life annuity is treated as containing a capital element and an income element. The capital element is tax free so only the income element is taxable as investment income. When paying over the income the life company is obliged to deduct income tax at the basic rate from the income element.

It may be possible to effect a capital protected annuity to provide some protection in the event of the early death of the annuitant.

4.14   HOME INCOME PLANS

These plans are aimed at elderly individuals with relatively little income who have mortgageable capital assets such as flats or houses in order that their net spendable income can be increased.

These plans allow an individual aged over 65 to utilize a high proportion of the value of the house to generate additional income while allowing him to remain in his home. The individual effectively borrows a proportion of the value of the house using the house as security for the loan and that loan is applied to purchase an annuity from a life office.

Part of the annuity must be used to pay the interest due on the loan and the balance provides additional income. The loan is not repaid until the death of the annuitant when the house may be sold to realize any funds necessary. Under these schemes the annuitant usually continues to benefit from the increase in value of his home but there are some schemes on the market where a proportional part automatically becomes the property of the life company in return for payment of a higher than usual level of annuity. Under some schemes commercial rates of interest are charged and higher levels of annuity are paid; under others a lower rate of annuity than usual is paid but is linked to lower interest rates charged on the loan.

As explained in 1.4.2, tax relief is available on the loan interest paid, provided that the loan does not exceed £30,000 and 90% is used to buy the annuity.

5 Provision for the Next Generation

5.1 TAX-EFFICIENT GIVING

As explained in 1.6.2, for transfers of assets made on or after March 1986, no charge to inheritance tax arises on lifetime gifts between individuals, or gifts into accumulation or maintenance trusts (see 5.2.2), interest in possession trusts (see 5.2.3) or trusts for the disabled. Consequently, an individual can give as much as he likes without there being a charge to inheritance tax provided, of course, that he survives seven years.

Generally, the advice must be that subject to providing sufficient funds for long-term needs the balance of one's estate, subject to commercial prudence, should be distributed now to the next or later generations either absolutely or by gift into qualifying settlements.

5.2 LIFETIME PLANNING USING SETTLEMENTS

Settlements generally can be a very effective tool in tax planning. Commercial considerations should always take precedence over the possible tax advantages to be gained, but nevertheless the latter do provide opportunities for some effective use to be made of lifetime transfers.

5.2.1 The discretionary settlement

This type of settlement allows the trustees power to distribute capital and income among the class of beneficiaries at their discretion, rather than on any fixed basis; alternatively the trustees can accumulate income.

The class of beneficiaries could include the settlor's spouse, children and grandchildren and other relatives or persons (such as charities). There could also be powers to add or exclude beneficiaries in the future.

Although the regime previously existing for discretionary trusts will substantially apply to new settlements one difference concerns the question of gifts with reservation considered in 1.6.2. A gift in excess of the *nil* rate band of currently £90,000 and annual exemptions into a discretionary trust will be taxable at half the rates set out in Appendix B. If the settlor is included in the class of beneficiaries, the assets in the settlement will be taxed as part of his estate on death. If the settlor excluded himself within seven years of death the tapered charge described at 1.6.1 will apply.

None the less, this type of settlement may still be useful. If a husband and wife wish to take advantage of the opportunity for tax-free gifts which may last until only the next general election, but wish to avoid making final decisions now, they should consider gifting assets within their *nil* rate bands and annual exemption into discretionary settlements prior to making any other gifts. This type of planning, however, should be followed only by those who have sufficient assets to give away part of their estate absolutely and give up any further benefit from that part.

The transfer of funds into the settlement is a transfer for *inheritance tax* purposes as described above. However, with the use of business property relief and the various exemptions described at 1.6.2 it is possible to transfer a substantial amount without incurring a liability to tax.

EXAMPLE 2

In 1987/88 Len transfers his 60% shareholding in Research Tax Limited, valued at £154,000, to a discretionary trust he has set up.

	£
Value of shares	192,000
Business property relief @ 50%	96,000
	96,000
Annual exemptions for two years	6,000
	£90,000

Provided Len has made no transfers of value for inheritance tax purposes in the past seven years, this amount will be within the *nil* rate band in the inheritance tax table (see Appendix B), so that no tax is chargeable.

If the transfer does give rise to a charge to inheritance

tax, this, if it is paid by the trustees, can usually be paid by ten interest-free annual instalments; this relief applies to most categories of assets which cannot be easily disposed of, for example unquoted shares. In turn this tax could be funded by the settlor making an annual gift to the trustees; if this is within his or her £3,000 annual exemption, there can still be no tax to pay.

There is a charge to inheritance tax on each tenth anniversary of the settlement. This is calculated on the value of the assets in the settlement and tax is charged at 15% of the normal inheritance tax rates. The maximum rate of tax payable in these circumstances is therefore 15% of 60%, i.e. 9%.

When a distribution takes place prior to the tenth anniversary, inheritance tax is charged (at the rates then in force) by reference to the value of the assets when they entered the settlement (ignoring business property relief). If this notional rate is *nil*, this still applies, even though the value at the date of distribution may be considerably greater.

So far as *capital gains tax* is concerned, this also applies on the transfer of assets to the settlement but any liability can be held over in accordance with the usual rules relating to gifts. Where a sale of shares is anticipated (and this could be particularly important in the case of a flotation on The Stock Exchange or the unlisted securities market) it may be possible to defer payment of any charge to CGT indefinitely by appointing non-resident trustees to the settlement. This will crystallize any earlier held-over gain, but this may be a small price to pay as the gains realized by the non-resident trustees will generally become chargeable in the UK only when the settlor or a member of his family receives capital from the settlement. Where the ultimate beneficiary is not UK domiciled and neither resident nor ordinarily resident in the UK when payment is made then this deferral may become permanent.

Where the settlor and/or his spouse are included in the class of beneficiaries, the income from such a settlement is treated as their income for *income tax* purposes, irrespective of whether it is paid to them. Otherwise the income is subject to a special rate of income tax, currently fixed at 45%.

5.2.2 The accumulation and maintenance settlement

This is a particular form of discretionary settlement which carries some peculiar advantages of its own; its format has already been described in 1.6.5. It is a settlement which does not include the settlor or his spouse as a beneficiary but instead concentrates on their children or grandchildren as the primary beneficiaries; an essential condition is that a beneficiary must at least become entitled to receive income from the settlement at an age no greater than 25 years. Capital can pass to the child at any time and it is usual to leave this aspect to the trustees' discretion.

In this situation no inheritance tax will arise on gifts made into it more than seven years before the settlor's death; the periodic charge mentioned above for discretionary trusts will not be payable, and no further tax will arise when a beneficiary attains his interest. The capital gains tax consequences are as described in 5.2.1 while income tax is charged only at the special rate of 45%, until a beneficiary becomes entitled to the income or a share of it. Should income be received by, or paid for the benefit of, a minor beneficiary, a tax charge will arise on the parent in situations where he is the settlor as described in 3.1.

5.2.3 The interest in possession settlement

Where a transfer into such a settlement (broadly one where there is a person entitled to receive the income from it) is made on or after 17 March 1987, again no tax will arise provided that the settlor survives for at least seven years from the date of making the transfer. Furthermore no immediate charge to tax arises where a beneficiary's interest comes to an end (though it remains potentially chargeable for seven years), if on that event one of the following situations applies:

(1) another individual obtains an interest in the trust, either in the capital or the income;
(2) the trust assets pass to an accumulation and mainten-ance settlement or to a trust for the disabled;
(3) the value of another individual's estate is increased.

These reliefs were not available for transfers into this kind of settlement made prior to 17 March 1987 and the position was as that described above for discretionary settlements.

Otherwise the assets of the trust are treated as part of the estate of a beneficiary entitled to income from it for the purpose of determining the tax payable on his death.

5.2.4   The personal settlement

Under this type of settlement the income would usually be payable to the settlor for life, then to his widow for life and thereafter to their children and/or other beneficiaries on fixed or discretionary trusts. The trustees could have power to pay capital to the settlor or his spouse/widow at any time.

In this situation, no inheritance tax would be payable on the transfer of assets into the settlement as their underlying value continues to be treated as part of the settlor's estate for inheritance tax purposes. Tax may arise subsequently, e.g. on the death of the settlor or of his widow, in accordance with the normal rules. The same capital gains tax consequences arise as described for discretionary settlements in 5.2.1.

Income tax continues to be charged on the income arising on the settlor in his lifetime and on his widow during her lifetime.

Exactly the same consequences flow if the trust is made by the wife leaving an interest to her widower on her death.

5.3   FUNDING THE ULTIMATE INHERITANCE TAX LIABILITY

There will be many estates where the ultimate inheritance tax liability payable on the death of the survivor of the individual and his wife will still be substantial irrespective of the amount of planning carried out during their lifetimes. In these situations consideration should be given to providing funds to meet part or all of the prospective inheritance tax liability, thereby preserving the assets of the estate for the beneficiaries. Some of the ways in which this can be facilitated are set out below.

5.3.1 Joint life and survivor policies

One method is for the husband and wife, who intend to leave their respective estates to their spouse, to take out a joint life and survivor policy, written in trust, on their lives so that on the death of the survivor (when the inheritance tax liability will crystallize) the policy proceeds will be payable free of all taxes to the beneficiaries. This will enable them to pay part or all of the inheritance tax liability, thereby preserving the assets then passing. The policy may be written on suitable trusts for the benefit of the intended beneficiaries.

Both spouses can be included in the class of beneficiaries and this enables the policy to be terminated in favour of either of them. While such a course of action will lose any inheritance tax benefit, it may nevertheless be comforting for the couple to know that either of them can recover the surrender value of the policy if their financial position deteriorates unexpectedly. The premiums on such policies will normally fall within the exemption for normal expenditure out of income.

A variation of this idea is where an elderly taxpayer purchases an annuity to improve his net spendable income and replaces the capital in his estate by taking out a life policy written in trust for his intended beneficiaries, the premiums being paid from the annuity income. The capital cost of the annuity is effectively removed from the estate and replaced by the insurance policy proceeds which are not liable to inheritance tax provided that the terms of the annuity and the life policies do not depend upon each other.

5.3.2　Death-in-service benefits

One of the benefits permitted by the Revenue in an occupational pension scheme (see 4.3) is, in the event of the employee's death in service, the payment of a tax-free lump sum of up to four times final salary and the return of his contributions plus interest. Both these benefits are usually payable at the discretion of the pension fund trustees and are consequently completely free of inheritance tax.

The individual should indicate to the trustees of the pension scheme how the death-in-service benefit is to be allocated in the event of his death. For example, he could set up a discretionary trust during his lifetime to receive the money. This could be for the benefit of his children or perhaps could be used to pay some or all of the eventual inheritance tax liability on his widow's death.

As indicated in 4.6, a self-employed person is able to invest a proportion of his retirement annuity premium payments (up to 5% of net relevant earnings) in a term assurance policy under which a lump sum will be payable in the event of death before retirement. The policy (and the death benefits payable under his normal retirement annuity policies) can be assigned into a discretionary trust so that the proceeds fall outside his estate for inheritance tax purposes in the event of death before retirement.

6 Making a Will

6.1 CONSEQUENCES OF NOT MAKING A WILL

It is very important to make a will. Not only does it ensure
that the way you wish your estate to be devolved upon
your death is known. There should also be no difficulties
where some beneficiaries turn out to be under age or
uncooperative. If a person dies without making a will his
estate will devolve under the rules of intestacy which are
generally inflexible and in many cases can actually cause
considerable hardship for the deceased's family. Furthermore, a well drawn up will can save tax.

To illustrate, the laws of intestacy provide that the
surviving widow or widower takes the following interests:

(a) *Personal chattels*. The surviving spouse will always be
     entitled to the personal chattels except in the situation
     where the estate is insolvent. The personal represen-
     tatives may sell them only where this is necessary to
     pay debts and expenses.

(b) *Residuary interests.* The balance of the estate to which the surviving spouse will be entitled will depend upon whether there are any other surviving relatives. Where there are any children or remoter issue the surviving spouse takes £75,000 and a life interest in one-half of the residue. If there is no issue but a parent or a brother or sister the surviving spouse is entitled to £125,000 and an absolute interest in half the residue. Where there are no other surviving relations the spouse takes the whole of the residue absolutely.

For instance, a shareholder who owns a significant stake in a private company will have to give special consideration to the manner in which the shares pass after his death. In some cases it may be correct for the shares to be passed outright to the shareholder's spouse; in other cases it may be more appropriate for the shares to be held in trust for the surviving spouse, leaving the trustees to make major decisions regarding the future of the company. In the latter case careful consideration needs to be given to the choice of trustees.

6.2 VARIATION OF THE TERMS OF A WILL

Great care is necessary where the beneficiaries of a deceased person's will (or on his intestacy) wish to vary the dispositions contained therein if the whole operation is not to fail. This may be achieved by a *deed of family arrangement.* There are a number of legal provisions that must be met:

(a) The variation must be made within two years following the death.

(b) It must apply to property held in the estate immediately before the death.

(c) The variation must be an instrument in writing made by the persons who benefit or who would benefit from the will.

(d) An election must be sent, signed by all the persons making the variation, to the Inland Revenue within six months after the deed has been executed, although in most situations personal representatives will not have to sign. The Revenue has discretion to extend this time limit.

(e) The variation or disclaimer must not be made for a consideration.

It is imperative that the appropriate words of variation or disclaimer appear in the deed itself because otherwise the Inland Revenue takes the view that it can have no inheritance tax effect.

The Revenue has also specified certain conditions which it considers must be satisfied before an instrument of variation can have effect for inheritance tax purposes in addition to the statutory provisions:

(i) The instrument must clearly indicate the dispositions that are the subject of it and vary their destination as laid down in the will or under the law of intestacy.

It is not necessary that the instrument should purport to vary the will or intestacy provisions themselves; it is sufficient if the instrument identifies the disposition to be varied and varies its destination.

(ii) The notice of election must refer to the appropriate statutory provisions.

(iii) Where there is more than one variation in relation to the same will or intestacy, the Revenue considers that an election validly made is irrevocable and that an instrument will not fall within the appropriate statutory section if it *further* redirects any item (or part of any item) that has already been redirected by an earlier instrument.

Where an election is not made, the deed will continue to be effective but will result in those parties to the deed giving up a benefit being treated as if they had made a lifetime transfer. Where the election is made no lifetime transfer results; the deceased is treated as having made the revised dispositions.

A similar but separate election needs to be made if there is to be no capital gains tax effect on the execution of the deed. When the election is made the provisions of the deed again relate back to the death and the new beneficiary takes them at their value on that date. Where no election is made for capital gains tax purposes the new beneficiary takes the assets at their value on the date of the deed instead of the date of death. There could be circumstances where this could be beneficial, for instance where the previous beneficiary can use part of his annual exemption for CGT purposes on a gain arising since the death and pass the asset at a higher base cost to the new beneficiary.

No equivalent election applies for income tax purposes. The rules here are that the income arising from the date of death to the date of the execution of the deed will be allocated to the beneficiaries as determined by the will. Where any beneficiary has become chargeable to tax and has paid that tax he is entitled to recover from the person to whom the income is actually payable the amount of the tax suffered.

One possible disadvantage in a person giving up an interest using a deed of variation is that he will be treated as being a settlor for tax purposes with the consequence that should an infant unmarried child of his benefit by his action any income arising from the asset concerned and paid or applied for that child's benefit will be treated as his income.

As a general point where a testator expresses a wish that property bequeathed by his will should be transferred to people other than the persons named in the will and the first beneficiary transfers any of that property in accordance with that wish within two years after the death of the testator the property will again be treated for inheritance tax purposes as having been transferred by the will to the ultimate beneficiary.

6.3 TWO-YEAR DISCRETIONARY WILL

There is now a modern form of will, known as the two-year discretionary will, which provides greater flexibility than a conventional will.

Under this type of will the testator bequeaths the residue of his estate on discretionary trusts for a two-year period and leaves it to his executors to distribute his estate within that period in accordance with a letter of wishes which he places with his will and updates from time to time to meet any changes in his wishes or circumstances.

Therefore, the executors will be able to distribute the estate in accordance with the testator's known wishes at the time of his death and also take advantage of any tax reliefs available at that time. This type of will is particularly useful where some equalization of estates has taken place between husband and wife. In the event of the untimely death of one spouse it enables the survivor to retrieve some of the assets previously transferred.

This type of will also overcomes the necessity of amendments to the will to meet changes in legislation and changes in family circumstances. Instead, the testator merely alters his letter of wishes. This approach is more flexible and far less complicated and costly, as can be appreciated from the process necessary to ensure an effective deed of variation described at 6.2.

6.4 SURVIVORSHIP CLAUSE

Most wills contain survivorship clauses which allow property left in a will to a beneficiary to be passed to him only on that beneficiary outliving the deceased by 30 days. The reason for this is that were the potential beneficiary to die in the same accident or very shortly afterwards there is little point in passing the asset to him and it would merely complicate matters.

Consequently, from the date of death until the end of the stated period has passed the property is held for the beneficiary but will be passed to him only on his surviving the conditional period. Technically the property is treated as being in a settlement but with no one entitled to receive the income therefrom. The disposition will finally take effect at the end of the stated period, or on the deceased's death if the beneficiary does not survive until then, but is treated as having had effect from the beginning of the period. Consequently, the inheritance tax liability will be calculated as though the beneficiary was entitled at the moment of death.

6.5 COMMORIENTES

Where a number of people are killed in an accident so that it is unknown who died first the general rule applied (known as the *law of commorientes*) is that the elder is treated as having died first. Consequently, any younger people killed in the accident could inherit assets from the elder individual because they are deemed to have died afterwards. Hence the importance of survivorship clauses as described in 6.4. Also an older individual cannot inherit any assets from a younger individual because of the general rule that a legacy must lapse if it is intended to be given to a person who predeceases the testator. Consequently where property passes from the older to the younger individual under these arrangements inheritance tax will be chargeable on the property concerned only on the first, i.e. the elder's, death.

7 Residence Abroad

7.1 INTRODUCTION

In these days of high mobility of labour, many individuals find themselves working abroad, either part time or full time, and the tax implications of doing so need to be considered carefully.

It is also increasingly common for individuals reaching retirement age, particularly where their more expensive family commitments have come to an end, to go and live abroad, perhaps where the climate and living conditions generally are more to their taste or where they have established connections from earlier visits. Here again tax can play an important part in the overall planning. However, it is essential that tax is *not* used as the prime reason for settling abroad, and the preferred retirement location must be congenial from all points of view.

7.2 NON-TAX CONSIDERATIONS

It must always be remembered that other countries have different laws and customs from those of the UK and an understanding of these is clearly important to anyone going overseas. It is particularly recommended that advice be sought on the following matters before entering a foreign country:

(a) the level of remuneration required to secure an adequate standard of living;
(b) visas and work permits;
(c) local exchange control regulations (these still apply in many overseas countries and the rules are often strict);
(d) banking arrangements (where residence is retained in the UK no special arrangements are usually necessary other than those required for the provision of funds needed for local living expenses);
(e) health regulations including inoculations;
(f) availability of housing and likely costs;
(g) import duties on household effects;
(h) availability of language courses;
(i) children's education;
(j) possible military service requirements;
(k) social customs and prohibitions;
(l) medical and dental costs;
(m) quarantine regulations for pets, both entering the country and returning to the UK;
(n) driving licences;
(o) adequacy of cover for life and other insurances while abroad.

7.3   DOMICILE AND RESIDENCE

The United Kingdom tax liability of an individual who is normally resident in the UK but who has an overseas employment can be affected by three factors: his *domicile*, *residence* status and *ordinary residence* status. These terms are not defined in the taxing statutes but are based on a substantial body of case law going back over many years and on Inland Revenue practice which has developed over that period.

7.3.1   Domicile

A person's 'domicile' is essentially the country which he looks on as his natural homeland. It is quite distinct from legal nationality and from residence. A person starts with a 'domicile of origin' which is normally his father's domicile; he retains this until he acquires a 'domicile of choice' which can be done only by severing his ties with the domicile of origin and producing evidence of a firm intention of settling permanently in another country. A person who is resident in the UK but domiciled overseas has certain tax advantages: he may be able to claim a deduction from his earnings if he has a foreign employer; and capital gains from overseas assets, dividends, interest and royalties from overseas, and income from overseas trades are taxed only in so far as they are remitted to the UK.

7.3.2 Residence and ordinary residence

For tax purposes residence and ordinary residence normally have to be decided for a tax year. An individual who has been habitually resident in the UK will be regarded as resident in this country if any absence abroad is purely temporary. 'Temporary' is defined as 'occasional'. This statutory definition would have made it difficult for a British subject to shed his 'residence' had it not been for an Inland Revenue concession described below.

'Ordinarily resident' means habitually resident. A person could in theory be ordinarily resident for a tax year for which he was absent from the UK for the whole year and therefore not resident – if, for example, he goes to Bermuda for a holiday and stays for a whole tax year. Similarly, it is possible for individuals to be resident but not ordinarily resident – for example if he normally lives overseas but happens to spend more than 183 days in the UK in a particular tax year (or even sets foot here at all, if he has a place of abode available for his use where an employment is not involved; see 7.3.4). Neither of these situations is likely to arise in the case of an individual going abroad for an extended period or permanently and for most purposes the distinction between residence and ordinary residence need not concern such an individual.

It is possible to be resident for tax purposes in more than one country, and a person cannot claim that he is not resident in the UK merely because he is resident somewhere else. However, some double tax treaties provide that a person can be resident only of one of the countries concerned for the purposes of the agreement, and the concept of residence is more narrowly defined in such agreements so as to avoid ambiguity.

Legally, a person is either resident or not resident for a whole tax year. However, by concession tax years may be split for this purpose. In particular, if a person goes abroad for full-time service under a contract of employment or to be self-employed full time, he will normally be treated as being not resident and not ordinarily resident from the day following his departure until the day before the date of his return. This applies if all the following conditions are satisfied:

(a) all the duties of the employment must be performed abroad or any duties performed in the UK must be only incidental to the overseas duties; *and*

(b) the absence from the UK in the employment must be for a period which includes a complete tax year; *and*

(c) interim visits to the UK, perhaps for holiday purposes, must not amount to more than six months in any one tax year or three months per year on average over four years.

For this purpose the overseas employment should be a new employment separate from the former employment in the UK.

7.3.3 Husband and wife

A wife's domicile status, while she is living with her husband, normally follows his. However, since 1 January 1974 it has been possible for a lady of overseas domicile who marries a man having UK domicile to contend that her overseas domicile continues; this does require that she can establish that her way of life does support an argument for an independent domicile, which in practice would be far from easy.

A wife's residence status is independent of that of her husband. If a man is employed full time abroad, and his wife goes with him but returns before she has been away for a complete tax year, she will remain resident in the UK. If the resident status of the spouses differ in this way, husband and wife are treated as separate individuals for UK tax purposes unless this is to their disadvantage.

This can introduce certain tax planning opportunities such as the execution of a deed of covenant (see 1.4.3) by the non-resident spouse in favour of the resident spouse provided certain conditions are met and the individual's circumstances allow it.

7.3.4 Available accommodation

If a person goes abroad other than for full-time employ-ment and has accommodation available for his use in the UK (whether he owns it or not), he is treated as resident in the UK for any tax year in which he sets foot in the UK at all. This rule does not apply to someone in full-time overseas employment or self-employment performing only incidental duties in the UK.

7.3.5 Procedure

Where an individual leaves the UK he is required to complete a questionnaire (form P85) so that the Revenue can give a provisional ruling as to his residence status. Professional advice should be sought in completing this form.

7.4 EMPLOYMENT EARNINGS

The provisions relating to the taxation in the UK of employment earnings are complex and beyond the scope of this book to cover in detail. The basic rules for domiciled individuals are set out below and summarized in the table on page 130. More information on this subject is given in *The Touche Ross Tax Guide to Pay and Perks 1987/88* by Bill Packer and Elaine Baker (Papermac, 1987).

Non-resident. Earnings are taxable in the UK only in so far as they are attributable to any duties of the employment which are performed in the UK. Where duties are carried out partly in the UK and partly overseas, it is strongly recommended that separate contracts of employment should be used and that their terms should be commercially justifiable.

Where duties are normally performed overseas, any incidental duties performed in the UK will be ignored.

Resident but not ordinarily resident. Earnings attributable to duties performed in the UK are taxable in full here; earnings attributable to duties performed abroad are taxable only on the remittance basis. Where the earnings are not specifically separated, the Inland Revenue is normally prepared to accept an apportionment of them between 'UK' and 'non-UK' on the basis of the number of days worked within and outside the UK in a tax year.

It is important that an individual in this situation who is paid abroad sets up separate bank accounts overseas so that any remittances he makes to the UK can be clearly identified.

Resident. Where such an individual spends at least 365 days working wholly or partly overseas, he may be entitled to the so-called *100% deduction*, so that his overseas earnings are not subject to tax in the UK, even though he is still regarded as resident in this country.

The 365-day qualification is modified to allow visits of limited duration to the UK and to cover leave periods.

Travelling expenses incurred in going out to an overseas posting and in returning from it and (since 6 April 1984) on unlimited trips to and from the UK in the course of it are not taxable as a benefit in kind where they are borne by the employer. This also applies to two return trips for spouse and children during the posting and to reasonable board and lodging paid for by the employer while the individual is overseas.

Collection of tax on overseas earnings. Where the employer is operating in the UK, PAYE is applied in the usual way. Where it is clear that the 100% deduction is applicable, a 'no tax' (NT) code is issued so that the employer may pay the relevant remuneration without deducting UK tax.

If the emoluments are paid overseas by an overseas employer who does not have a branch office or base in

UK tax liability on employment earnings – employer resident in the UK, employee domiciled in the UK

Employee's residence status	Duties performed					
		Partly abroad			Wholly abroad	
	Wholly in UK 1	Partly in UK 2	Absent less than 365 days 3	Absent 365 days or more (continuous period) not incidental to UK duties 4	Absent less than 365 days 5	Absent 365 days or more (continuous period) 6
Resident and ordinary resident	All	All subject to columns 3 and 4	All of that part	None	All	None
Resident but NOT ordinarily resident	All	That part	Remittances from overseas part	Remittances from overseas part	Remittances	Remittances
NOT resident	All	That part	None	None	None	None

this country, PAYE cannot be applied, and tax will have to be charged by direct assessment on the employee under what is known as the direct collection ('DC') procedure. A provisional assessment is made early in the tax year on the individual, computing his liability to UK income tax on an estimate of his taxable income in that year, and this provisional liability is collected from the taxpayer normally in four instalments. After the end of the year when the exact amount of taxable income is known, the assessment is adjusted accordingly. If this gives rise to further tax, this is collected from the individual; if he is found to have paid too much tax, the excess is either refunded to him or set against his liability for the following year.

National insurance contributions. If an individual working overseas remains on his UK employer's payroll, national insurance contributions at the Class 1 rate continue to be payable. After the first 12 months the individual may opt to pay contributions at the voluntary Class 3 rate. If the individual is employed by an overseas employer who does not have a place of business in the UK, Class 1 contributions cannot be paid but he can elect at the start of his overseas tour to pay Class 3 contributions to preserve his retirement pension benefits.

Many countries (including all EEC member countries and the United States) have reciprocal arrangements with the UK. Advice should be obtained from any office of the Department of Health and Social Security prior to working overseas for an overseas employer, or for more than one year for a UK employer, so as to ensure that the correct amount and type of contributions are paid.

7.5   TAX ON OTHER INCOME OF NON-RESIDENTS

7.5.1   UK source income

Basically a non-resident is taxable in the UK on all income from sources within the UK, except that interest on certain designated UK government securities is exempt from tax if the owner is not ordinarily resident here. As to whether the exemption applies to any particular stock is always specified in the official prospectus relating to that stock.

An individual letting out his house in the UK is taxed on the rental income, subject to deductions for rates, insurance, repairs, etc. Relief at the income tax basic rate for mortgage interest paid will normally be given by deduction at source under the MIRAS arrangement; any relief due at higher tax rates will be given directly by assessment. If rent is paid from the UK to a person whose usual place of abode is overseas, tax at the basic rate has to be deducted. If such rent is paid through an agent in the UK, the agent can be assessed to the tax, which he will withhold before passing the rent to the recipient overseas. This will not apply to an individual overseas for a limited period only. The recipient has to claim repayment if any of the rental income is covered by reliefs to which he is entitled, e.g. a proportion of part of his personal allowances (see 7.6) or relief for mortgage interest payable.

7.5.2   Non UK source income

In general a non-resident is not liable to UK tax on income from overseas sources. As mentioned in 1.3.4, if foreign dividends and interest are paid through a bank or paying agent in the UK, the bank or agent normally has to deduct tax at the basic rate when paying over the income. A non-resident can reclaim tax or arrange for the income to be paid gross but this is possible only if his absence from the UK is likely to be for at least three years.

7.6 PERSONAL ALLOWANCES FOR NON-RESIDENTS

Personal reliefs for UK income tax are basically available only to a UK resident, but certain categories of non-resident can claim a proportion of them. To be eligible for the relief the non-resident must be

(a) a British subject (including Commonwealth subjects) or a citizen of the Irish Republic; *or*

(b) a person who is or has been in the service of the Crown; *or*

(c) a person employed in the service of any missionary society; *or*

(d) a person employed in the service of any territory under Her Majesty's protection; *or*

(e) a resident of the Channel Islands or the Isle of Man; *or*

(f) a former UK resident who is resident abroad for the sake of his health or the health of a member of his family resident with him; *or*

(g)   a widow whose late husband was in Crown service; or

(h)   a resident and/or national of a country with which the UK has a double tax treaty providing specifically for the relief. These countries currently are:

Austria	Irish Republic	Norway
Belgium	Italy	Portugal
Burma	Kenya	Singapore
Faroe Islands	Luxembourg	South Africa
Fiji	Mauritius	Swaziland
Finland	Namibia	Sweden
France	Netherlands	Switzerland
Greece	Netherlands	West Germany
Indonesia	Antilles	Zambia

A British woman married to a national of another country cannot claim as a British subject under (a), as claims are dealt with by reference to the husband's status.

The calculation of the relief is complicated; its value in terms of tax depends on the actual amounts of UK-taxable income and of world income. The tax that would be payable on the world income is calculated as if it were all taxable, and the resultant tax is reduced by the fraction:

$$\frac{\text{UK-taxable income}}{\text{world income}}$$

This figure is the *minimum* amount of tax payable, ignoring any double taxation relief.

EXAMPLE 3

David and Anne are British subjects resident in Australia in the tax year 1987/88 where David works. They own a house in England which is let. Anne receives £3,000 from a trust in the UK. Their UK tax liability would be calculated as follows:

	World income £	UK-taxable income £
David's salary	28,000	—
Trust income	3,000	3,000
Rental income (after expenses, UK mortgage interest, etc.)	1,000	1,000
	32,000	£4,000
Less Personal allowance	3,795	
	£28,205	

Tax chargeable on £28,205 is £9,485.

On claiming under these provisions, the UK tax cannot be reduced below:

$$\frac{4,000}{32,000} \times £9,485 = £1,185$$

The calculation is modified if an individual's income includes UK source income which bears a reduced rate of

UK tax because of a double tax treaty, for example, dividends, interest and royalties. (This does not mean income which is *exempt* from UK tax under a treaty, or income in respect of which tax credit is available – there has to be a limit on the rate of UK tax which can be charged.) The calculation is modified as follows:

(a) Omit the income eligible for double tax relief in calculating the income tax payable.
(b) Omit the income eligible for double tax relief from income subject to UK tax.
(c) Include the income eligible for double tax relief in total world income and in calculating the hypothetical tax on that income without regard to double tax relief.

The tax payable by the individual cannot, in any case, be higher than it would have been if the double tax relief had not been available.

EXAMPLE 4

Bill and Lorraine are British subjects resident in France in the tax year 1987/88, where Bill works. Bill receives £1,000 per year loan stock interest from the UK, and Lorraine receives £3,000 from a UK trust. Under the UK/France double tax treaty, UK tax on the interest is limited to 10% (provided that it is taxable in France). The UK tax would be calculated as follows:

	World income	*UK-taxable income*
	£	£
Bill's salary	28,000	—
Trust income	3,000	3,000
Interest	1,000	—
	32,000	£3,000
Personal allowance	3,795	
	£28,205	

Tax chargeable on £28,205 is £9,485.

On claiming under these provisions, the UK tax cannot be reduced below:

$$\frac{3,000}{32,000} \times £9,485 = £889$$

(If double tax relief on the interest received had not been available, the UK tax would have been £1,185 as in Example 3.)

Where the individual has already suffered UK tax by deduction at source or otherwise in excess of his due liability computed as above, he can normally claim repayment of the excess.

7.7 DOUBLE TAXATION RELIEF

If any income of a UK resident is taxed both in the UK and in an overseas country, relief may be claimed, in all or in part, from the UK tax either under a double tax treaty or under UK tax rules which provide relief in cases where it is not provided for in an agreement ('unilateral relief'). The details are complex and beyond the scope of this book.

When emoluments in respect of which overseas tax has been paid are also taxable in the UK, credit will be given for overseas tax against the UK tax arising from that source. If the overseas tax exceeds the UK tax on those earnings, the tax credit is normally restricted to the UK tax. Where the 100% deduction applies (7.4) no credit can be claimed because the UK tax liability from that source will be nil and there is therefore no doubly taxed income.

7.7.1 Employment earnings

In the case of non-residents most double tax treaties with other countries provide exemption from UK tax on earnings from employment performed in the UK by a person who is resident in the other country for the purposes of the treaty under certain conditions. The three basic conditions are usually:

(a) that the employer is, or that the services are performed on behalf of, a resident of the other country; *and*
(b) that the person is not present in the UK for more

than 183 days in the tax year; *and*

(c) that the earnings are not borne as such by any UK permanent establishment of the employer.

7.7.2 Other income

Under many double tax treaties non-residents are given relief from UK-source income. The treaties vary considerably and it is beyond the scope of this book to describe the differences between the treaties in detail. Some relief is usually provided from UK tax on independent professional services, dividends, interest, royalties and pensions and purchased annuities.

Income from independent professional services is normally taxed only in the country of residence unless the person concerned has a fixed base in the UK. Professional services include independent scientific, literary, artistic, educational or teaching activities as well as the services of doctors, lawyers, engineers, architects, dentists and accountants. This exemption is not usually available to entertainers or athletes who, since 1 May 1987, have been subject to special procedures for the collection of tax attributable to activities taking place in the UK.

Since 1973, when the imputation system for taxing UK dividends was introduced (see 1.3.3), the UK has been renegotiating all its double tax treaties to take account of the new system. The renegotiated treaties usually provide for non-resident shareholders of UK companies to be entitled to some or all of the tax credit: in the UK/France agreement, for instance, a shareholder who is resident in France and subject to French tax on the dividend will be paid a tax credit equal to the full ACT credit available to a resident shareholder less 15% of the dividend plus the credit.

EXAMPLE 5

	£
Dividend paid to shareholder	£73
ACT payable	27
Less: 15% of 73 + 27 = 100	15
Shareholder entitled to credit of	£12

UK tax on interest arising in the UK and paid to a non-resident is usually limited to low rates, up to 15%, frequently nil. Royalties are treated in the same way, with the rate generally being low, frequently nil.

Some treaties specifically recognize the right to tax income from real property in the country where the property is situated. There is usually no provision for any relief in the other country.

Pensions (except UK government pensions) and purchased annuities can usually be taxed only in the country of residence. Government pensions (that is, pensions paid out of public funds) are commonly exempt from tax in the country of residence but fully taxed in the country where payment arises.

7.7.3 The UK's double tax treaties

The UK has comprehensive double tax treaties with the following countries:

Antigua
Aruba
Australia
Austria
Bangladesh
Barbados
Belgium
Belize
Botswana
Brunei
Burma
Canada
China
Cyprus
Denmark
Egypt
Falkland Islands
Faroe Islands
Fiji
Finland
France
Gambia
Ghana
Greece
Grenada
Guernsey &
   Alderney
Hungary
India

Indonesia
Irish Republic
Isle of Man
Israel
Italy
Ivory Coast
Jamaica
Japan
Jersey
Kenya
Kiribati
Lesotho
Luxembourg
Malawi
Malaysia
Malta
Mauritius
Montserrat
Morocco
Namibia
Netherlands
Netherlands
   Antilles
New Zealand
Norway
Pakistan
Philippines
Poland
Portugal

Romania
St Christopher
   and Nevis
   (St Kitts)
Sierra Leone
Singapore
Solomon Islands
South Africa
South Korea
Spain
Sri Lanka
Sudan
Swaziland
Sweden
Switzerland
Thailand
Trinidad and
   Tobago
Tunisia
Tuvalu
Uganda
United States of
   America
USSR
West Germany
Yugoslavia
Zambia
Zimbabwe

7.8   UNREMITTABLE OVERSEAS INCOME

If an individual cannot remit any overseas income to the UK because of the operation of the law in the overseas country concerned or because of the executive action of its government or because the necessary foreign exchange is unobtainable, he can claim to postpone any UK tax liability on the income until it can be remitted here or brought out in any other way, e.g. by conversion into some other remittable foreign currency. Liability to UK taxation arises by reference to when the income can be remitted and not when it is actually remitted.

8 Redundancy and Unemployment

8.1 TERMINATION PAYMENTS

8.1.1 Introduction

To most people the possible receipt of a lump sum payment on the termination of employment could be an attractive proposition, dependent on the size of the payment of course, but particularly because of the beneficial way in which such payments are usually taxed. However, it is dangerous to assume that all lump sum payments arising on the termination of employment will be taxed in this way; depending on the circumstances surrounding the payment it is not inconceivable that a full charge to tax will arise.

It is appropriate to look first at the circumstances where no exemption is available. The statutory definition of 'emoluments' is 'all salaries, fees, wages, perquisites and profits whatsoever'. This definition therefore excludes a 'capital' sum as income tax is a tax on income. However, the Inland Revenue has successfully contended that a payment is not 'capital' merely because it is relatively large. The decision is essentially a question of fact (see 8.1.2).

If the payments are in fact 'emoluments' an income tax liability will arise in full with no special relief. If the payments are *not* 'emoluments' they would have been tax free had it not been for specific legislation which prescribes how such sums are to be taxed. Even then three basic considerations arise:

(a) Certain payments may be exempt from tax altogether (see 8.1.3).
(b) The first part of the lump sums may be exempt (see 8.1.4).
(c) After taking into account (a) and (b) above the remainder of the sums received may be taxed at a reduced rate (see 8.1.4).

The above basic principles apply to the taxation of a majority of the lump sum payments commonly encountered in practice such as *ex gratia* payments, payments for commuting pension rights, redundancy payments and compensation for unfair dismissal or for loss of office. Special considerations apply to the following:

(i) payments for restrictive covenants (see 8.3);
(ii) payments for variation of service agreements (see 8.4);
(iii) payments for inducing an individual to give up employment (see 8.5).

Unless otherwise stated, what follows applies to all employees and directors.

Long-service awards are dealt with at 8.7.

It is the *date of termination*, i.e. when the office or employment comes to an end, that is relevant, not the date of payment.

8.1.2 Capital or income?

Since this is a question of fact, each case has to be considered on its merits. The following guidelines should be noted, but as with many areas of tax legislation, the list is not exhaustive and no one factor or piece of evidence may be regarded as conclusive:

(a) A payment in accordance with a contractual commitment (e.g. as specified in the individual's employment contract or, as in the case of directors of family companies, as laid down in the company's articles of association) will almost certainly be taxable as an emolument.

(b) A payment in recognition of past services will be taxed in full as additional remuneration for those services. Care is clearly necessary in the documentation relating to any termination payment to ensure that the Revenue cannot contend that it falls into this category. Recognition of the individual's personal qualities and business acumen should not invite attack. Wherever possible no formal decision to make any *ex gratia* payment should be recorded as being taken until after the employee has left the employer's service.

(c) Similarly a payment associated with any commitment by an individual as to his future role or relationship with the employer may be regarded as advance remuneration, i.e. in respect of services to be performed in the future. Consequently, it is better to pay a lump sum on or after termination of employment unconditionally rather than to pay the same sum on an understanding, either verbal or written, such as that the employee will assist his successor from time to time after his employment has ceased. Likewise care is necessary if the employee is to be paid a lump sum (on retirement or resignation from the employment) and is subsequently engaged as a 'consultant' or in some other capacity.

(d) As evidence of the precise terms of understanding and the nature of payments, the Inland Revenue may require to see all documentation and it is as well therefore for draft documents to be scrutinized and settled beforehand. This is of application to such documents as board minutes, internal memoranda and letters exchanged between the parties.

8.1.3 Exempt lump sums

The following lump sums are exempt from tax altogether:

(a) Death benefits and sums in respect of injury or disability (the Revenue have stated that 'disability' covers not only a condition resulting from a sudden affliction but also continuing incapacity to perform the duties of an office or employment arising out of the culmination of a process of deterioration of physical or mental health caused by chronic illness).

(b) Payments from approved pension schemes for part-commutation of pensions.

(c) Amounts used to acquire further benefits under an approved pension scheme provided the benefits are within the limits provided by the pension scheme. A similar exemption will apply to the purchase of an annuity for the employee as long as the transaction is of a type approved under the law.

(d) Payments made where there has been a substantial element of foreign service. This applies where the foreign service comprised either three-quarters of the whole period of service or the whole of the last ten years or where the period of service exceeded 20 years, one-half of the period including any ten of the last 20 years.

'Foreign service' broadly requires the recipient to have been not ordinarily resident in the UK and is likely to include a situation where the taxpayer was living with his family overseas.

8.1.4 The charge to tax

Lump sum payments which are not taxable in full as 'emoluments' on termination of employment are exempt to the extent of the first £25,000. This exemption is in addition to the sums exempted in 8.1.3.

This does not apply to payments for restrictive covenants (8.3), variation of service agreements (8.4) and inducing an individual to give up employment (8.5).

The aim of the legislation was to tax amounts payable after 6 April 1982 in excess of £25,000 as follows:

(a) *Part of payment between £25,000 to £50,000:* the relief is ½ × (tax payable if the whole of the taxable payment is charged as additional income less the tax payable ignoring the lump sum).

(b) *Part of payment between £50,000 and £75,000:* the relief is that applicable to a payment of £50,000 plus ¼ × (tax payable if the whole of the taxable payment is charged as additional income less the tax payable had the sum been exactly £50,000).

(c) *Part of payment over £75,000:* no further relief beyond that available for a payment of exactly £75,000.

The following example illustrates this.

EXAMPLE 6

Mr T. Rend has his employment terminated in 1987/88 and receives a lump sum payment of £90,000. His income and allowances are as follows:

	£	£
Earnings from employment	45,000	
Other income	2,000	
Lump sum termination payment	90,000	
Personal allowance	3,795	

Liability excluding lump sum:

	£	£
Earnings	45,000	
Other income	2,000	
	47,000	
Personal allowance	3,795	
Taxable income	£43,205	
Tax liability		£17,581

Liability on lump sum:

	£	£
Lump sum	90,000	
Exempt	25,000	
	£65,000	
Tax on £25,000 at 60%	15,000	
Reduced by half	7,500	7,500
Tax on £25,000 at 60%	15,000	
Reduced by a quarter	3,750	11,250
Tax on balance of £15,000 at 60%		9,000
Tax liability		£27,750
Total tax liability		£45,331

As explained above, it was the intention, when the rates were changed in 1982, that the treatment set out above should apply to termination payments treated as being received after 5 April 1982. However it has now been realized that the effect of the legislation as originally drafted was to tax the excess of the lump sum over the first £25,000 as follows:

next £50,000   – tax reduced by a half
next £25,000   – tax reduced by a quarter
excess over £100,000 – no reduction in tax

The legislation has now been amended, in relation to payments treated as received on or after 4 June 1986, to 'reinstate' the treatment originally intended; however this change is not to be applied retrospectively. Consequently, because the tax relief given on any lump sum exceeding £50,000 treated as paid during this period will have been calculated incorrectly, anyone who has paid tax on such a lump sum may now be entitled to make a supplementary claim for relief and to receive a repayment of tax. This could amount to as much as £7,500 (i.e. half of £25,000 at 60%) plus repayment supplement.

Supplementary claims may be made at any time within the period of six years from the end of the tax year in which the lump sum was treated as received.

8.1.5   PAYE

A lump sum payment on the cessation of employment is treated as pay for PAYE purposes to the extent that the payment exceeds £25,000.

Where a payment is made to an employee after he has left and been issued with Form P45 tax should be deducted from the amount exceeding £25,000 at the basic rate.

If the payment is made before Form P45 is issued the excess over £25,000 is included as pay on the deduction working sheet and the PAYE tables applied as normal.

However, because of the top-slicing provisions it is probable that excess tax may be deducted. If this is to be avoided the Inspector of Taxes should be notified of:

(a) the amount of the termination payment and the proposed date of payment;
(b) the total pay and tax deducted;
(c) the amount of any further pay due to the end of the employment and the proposed date of payment.

If this is done in time, it should be possible to agree a provisional amount to be deducted from the termination payment to take account of the top-slicing relief.

If this procedure is not followed and excess tax has been deducted and it is not possible to determine the employee's final tax liability for the year, it is Revenue practice to allow a provisional repayment claim of 75% of the estimated tax overpaid. After the end of the tax year the position is reviewed and any further repayment due is made.

Where an employer makes a termination payment in excess of £25,000 in a tax year he must supply the Revenue with full details of the payment within 30 days of the end of that tax year.

8.2 REDUNDANCY PAYMENTS

Statutory redundancy payments are exempt from income tax under Schedule E with the exception of any liability under the provisions taxing lump sum payments (see 8.1).

An employer is required to make this type of payment where he dismisses a worker wholly or mainly because he has ceased, or intends to cease, to carry on business for which the employee was employed or in the place where the employee was employed. These rules also apply where the employee is no longer required to carry out particular functions because that type of work has ceased or diminished, or is expected to do so. However, to qualify under these provisions the employee must have two years' continuous service with his employer but any period of service prior to the employee's 18th birthday does not count.

The Employment Acts provide for the following redundancy payments to be made:

(a) One and a half weeks' pay for each year of employment during which the employee was aged 41 to 64 years inclusive for men and 41 to 59 years inclusive for women.

(b) One week's pay for each year of employment during which the employee was aged 22 to 40 years inclusive.

(c) One-half of a week's pay for each year of employment in which the employee was aged 18 to 21 years inclusive.

Usually, only complete years are taken into account in calculating the payment although any year during part of which the employee was in a higher age group counts towards service in the age group immediately below. Qualifying service for these purposes is also limited to the last 20 years prior to the redundancy and, with effect from

1 April 1987, earnings above £158 per week are not taken into account.

The maximum payment possible under the scheme is £4,740 (£158 × 20 × 1½).

Non-statutory redundancy payments may be taxable in full if the payments are a condition of the employment or the employees expect such payments.

The Revenue has recently clarified the conditions under which the £25,000 exemption and the top-slicing relief will be given against non-statutory redundancy payments:

(a) The redundancy must be genuine.
(b) The employee must have been continuously in the service of the employer for at least two years.
(c) The payments are not made to selected employees only.
(d) The payments are not excessive in relation to earnings and length of service.

If an employer proposes to make such payments without deducting tax the arrangements should be cleared, in advance, with the PAYE Inspector of Taxes.

8.3 RESTRICTIVE COVENANTS

There are special provisions concerning the taxation of a payment by an employer to an employee in return for the employee undertaking to restrict his own business activities in direct competition with the business of the employer. It is not essential that such a payment is made on the termination of an employment, although in practice this is more common than for such a payment to be made at the commencement of, or during the currency of, the employment.

A payment in respect of restrictive covenants is normally regarded as being expenditure on enhancing goodwill and as far as the payer is concerned will qualify for relief only against capital gains on the sale of the business.

As regards the recipient, the tax liability is computed by 'grossing up' the sum received at the basic rate of tax and assessing higher rate tax only on the grossed sum (i.e. giving credit for the notional basic rate tax included in the grossing up).

EXAMPLE 7

The position where a 60% rate taxpayer received a payment of £150,000 would be as follows:

	£
Proposed payment	150,000
Grossing addition at 27%	55,479
Notional gross	£205,479
Tax thereon at 60%	123,287
Less Notional tax at 27% as above	55,479
Excess liability due by employee	£67,808
Effective rate of tax 67,808 ÷ 150,000	45.21%

Other points to note in considering a payment for restrictive covenants are:

(a) In certain circumstances, the Inland Revenue may argue that a payment on termination was for past services or that a payment on commencement was for future services (see 8.1.2). It is therefore strongly recommended that arrangements for such payments are clearly set out in writing, and professional advice should be sought.

(b) The employer must provide the Inland Revenue with details of such payments by 5 May following the end of the tax year in which the payments are made.

(c) Since such payments are disallowed in computing the employer's liability to tax, any tax planning in this area should carefully consider the position if the same sums had been paid as additional salary.

One other point needs to be observed. It is a necessary condition to be within the legislation that the sum paid will not otherwise fall to be treated as the income of any person for income tax purposes. Obviously the only person for whom this could be treated as income would be the employee himself; and the only way in which it could be treated as the employee's income would be if it could be assessable on him under Schedule E as remuneration of his employment. It is necessary to show that any payment is *not* a payment to the employee in respect of the performance by him of the duties of his employment. It would therefore be a payment to him not to perform certain acts which would be inimical to the performance of those duties or which he might be in a position to perform subsequent to the termination of the employment concerned.

8.4 VARIATION OF SERVICE AGREEMENTS

There are practical difficulties in deciding whether a particular payment is in respect of past or future services (see 8.1.2), or altogether exempt from tax. Perhaps it is useful to summarize briefly the decisions in two important cases on this subject:

(a) A payment of £40,000 was made to an employee in return for accepting a lower rate of remuneration in future. The duties of the employee remained essentially the same prior and subsequent to that payment and the entire sum fell to be taxed as income in the year of receipt.

(b) An employer company paid £10,000 to an individual in return for his resignation as chairman (he continued to serve as a director) and the payment was held to be capital. Considerable weight was attached to the fact that there *was* an alteration in the nature of duties and that he agreed not to pursue any contingent claim for compensation on relinquishing his chairmanship.

In the right circumstances it would appear to be open to an employer to pay a lump sum to an employee if he were demoted or given a less responsible job, etc. The case would be particularly strong if the employee could have had legal remedies under the employment legislation or perhaps a claim for unfair discrimination. However, the point is by no means clear cut and professional advice should be sought.

8.5 'GOLDEN HELLOS' AND 'HANDCUFFS'

8.5.1 'Hellos'

Where an individual has qualities and experience that a prospective employer considers would prove most valuable in his business the latter may consider sweetening an offer of employment with a cash lump sum payment or other valuable consideration. If it can be shown that the inducement arises from the office or employment the payment will comprise an emolument and be assessable under the normal provisions of Schedule E. If it cannot be classified as an emolument the inducement payment will incur no liability unless it can be brought within the termination payments provisions (see 8.1.2). This would, of course, depend on the circumstances but is not likely.

Cases considered by the courts show that in determining whether an inducement payment is to be regarded as an emolument one must carefully consider the facts. If it can be shown that something of value, e.g. status or future commission payments, is being given up and compensated for no tax liability may arise. However, if there are no significant considerations of this nature and the moneys involved can be seen to be advance remuneration the payment will attract a tax liability. The evidence is crucial. Clearly, the importance of findings of *fact* by the General or Special Commissioners in the early stages should not be underestimated because normally only if the Commissioners have erred in *law* will a court change their findings.

8.5.2 'Handcuffs'

There are a number of instances when it suits a purchaser who has incurred substantial sums of money in investing in new businesses or acquiring established businesses to enter into arrangements whereby the key individuals in the particular operation are encouraged to remain with the business. They are therefore available not only to assist in the change-over period but also to participate in the continued success of the business.

These arrangements can take many forms and will, inevitably, be a reflection of the particular circumstances found in any business take-over situation.

Some examples are as follows:

(a)   Deferred consideration – the purchaser can make arrangements to pay further sums of money to the vendor at some point in the future provided the vendor continues to take an active role in the business. Should the vendor decide to leave prior to the date that these arrangements would take effect from he forfeits any entitlement to further consideration.

(b) Loan notes – this is a variant of the deferred consideration route. In this situation the purchaser would promise to issue loan notes to the vendor on a particular date. That date would be the issue date of the loan notes and there may be adverse capital gains tax consequences.

(c) Pension schemes – so as to secure the continued efforts of staff who may not benefit from the disposal proceeds received from the business it may be appropriate to enter into arrangements whereby at a pre-arranged date in the future sums of money may be paid into pension schemes for the benefit of key employees. Such a payment should be tax deductible in the hands of the payer and should attract no tax liability in the hands of the employee.

(d) Discretionary settlements – under these arrangements a discretionary settlement is set up into which, perhaps on an annual basis, the new employer places sums of money for the benefit of a class of beneficiaries which will include key employees. Provided those employees remain with the firm for a specified period of time they may become entitled, at some time in the future, to a share of any distributions made at the discretion of the trustees. It is unlikely that these payments can escape a liability to tax under Schedule E in the usual way. It may also be possible by this means to achieve some saving of national insurance contributions. Whether or not these arrangements are commercially acceptable to the employees concerned is another question.

8.6   THE EMPLOYER'S POSITION

When one is considering the tax consequences of a lump sum payment in the hands of the employee one must also have regard to the employer's tax position because tax relief for the payer need not be automatic. The resulting consequences can be dramatic where the company is a family trading company making payments to family members.

Where the payer is a company one must first ensure that the proposed payment is not ultra vires, i.e. beyond the power of the company to make. Apart from a review of the objects clause of the memorandum of association three tests have been laid down by the courts for establishing whether a corporate gift is within the company's powers. To be valid any payment must be:

(a)   for the benefit of the company; *and*
(b)   reasonably incidental to its business; *and*
(c)   made bona fide in the interests of the company.

Normally, however, there should be little difficulty in ensuring that a payment is allowable in computing profits if the payment can be shown to be wholly and exclusively for the purposes of the trade. This can be shown to be the case where a payment is made:

(a)   to maintain the goodwill of the rest of the staff who can see that retiring employees are treated well;

(b)   because the trade can be more effectively carried on without the services of the dismissed employee.

Difficulties do arise, however, when payments are made that can in any way be connected with a cessation or sale of the business. Statutory redundancy payments under the Employment Protection (Consolidation) Act 1978 are allowable for tax purposes but where the trade is ceasing it must be impossible to prove that any payment made in this connection is wholly and exclusively for the purposes of the trade if the payment is made after the trade has ceased or shortly before.

Consequently the government introduced legislation in the 1980 Finance Act to alleviate this problem. As a result, payments in addition to the statutory redundancy payments made on a cessation of trading will be allowed on the same basis as would have applied had there been no cessation. The maximum allowance is up to three times the statutory redundancy payment. Where the payment is made after cessation it is treated as being paid on the last day business was carried on. These provisions will also apply to partial cessations where an identifiable activity or part of a trade is being discontinued.

The other area of difficulty is where the trade or business is being sold. As regards employees generally the above considerations will apply except where the payments are large. However, where a company terminated existing service agreements and paid compensation, the payments were disallowed on the grounds that they were connected with the sale and not the trade. Where the controlling shareholders receive a termination payment in connection with the sale of their company shareholding the Revenue may take an even tougher line. In one case immediately before the directors and sole shareholders of the company disposed of their shares an extraordinary meeting of the company was held at which a resolution was passed voting them £3,000 each as compensation for loss of office. The Revenue successfully contended that these payments were not deductible in arriving at the company's tax liability and that they were distributions of profit. If a company was to be in the same situation today this could give rise to a charge to ACT on the company and to higher rate tax on the shareholders (depending on their circumstances).

8.7　LONG-SERVICE AWARDS

Tax is not charged in respect of long-service awards provided that:

(a) the award is not in cash but in the form of tangible articles of reasonable cost, including shares in the employing company or in another company in the same group; *and*

(b) the cost to the employer is less than £20 per year of service; *and*

(c) the relevant period of service is at least 20 years and no similar award has been made to the same employee in the previous ten years.

8.8 UNEMPLOYMENT BENEFIT

To qualify for unemployment benefit the claimant must be unemployed but he must be not only capable of, but available for, work and all the qualifying conditions must be satisfied. Where he has voluntarily left his previous employment without good reason or refused to accept suitable employment or to attend an appropriate training course, he may be refused benefit for up to 13 weeks. The benefit is payable for a total of 39 weeks. However, subject to the 13-week rule above, benefit is not paid for the first three days of unemployment in any circumstances. Claims for benefit should be made immediately the individual becomes unemployed as payments cannot be made for days earlier.

After 4 July 1982 tax repayments are not made to the unemployed or strikers receiving taxable social security benefits. Instead, the Department of Employment maintains a record of the claimant's previous cumulative pay and tax details in the particular tax year and of all benefit paid to him. When the period of benefit claim ceases the claimant's tax position is recalculated; any repayment of tax due to him is made and a Form P45 is issued in the normal way to be given to the new employer.

9 Separation and Divorce

9.1 INTRODUCTION

This is a very difficult time for both parties but it is essential, especially where children are involved, to ensure that the maximum advantages offered by the tax system are obtained. The main tax objectives in any financial settlement relating to separation or divorce must be to ensure that:

(a) the party paying maintenance, mortgage interest, etc. receives full income tax relief;

(b) payments for the maintenance or education of any children are treated as the children's income for taxation purposes;

(c) capital gains tax is not payable on chargeable assets transferred;

(d) inheritance tax is not payable in the future on any assets transferred;

(e) *ad valorem* stamp duty is avoided where possible on assets transferred.

Provided the financial arrangements are carefully planned,

taking into account the circumstances of the individuals involved, material benefits can ensue.

9.2 INCOME TAX

Any marriage may end by death, divorce or separation which for income tax purposes is when the parties to the marriage cease 'living together'.

The relevant date for income tax purposes is the date of separation (*not* the date of divorce) and it is very important that this date is agreed by the parties at the outset. Husband and wife are treated separately for income tax purposes from the date of permanent separation. Thus in the year of separation the husband will be taxed on his own income plus the income of his wife up to the date of separation. The wife will be taxed as a single person from the date of separation.

9.2.1 Personal allowances

In the year of separation the husband is entitled to the full married man's allowance plus the wife's earned income allowance, if appropriate, as the income of the wife up to the date of the ending of the marriage is deemed to be his for tax purposes. The wife is entitled to the full single personal allowance against her income from the time the marriage ends to the following 5 April. There is no reduction in the married man's allowance by reference to the date of separation comparable to that which applies in the year of marriage. In the years following separation each spouse will be entitled only to the single person's allowance (subject to either remarrying). However, should the husband voluntarily continue wholly to maintain his wife he will go on receiving the married man's allowance. This is unlikely to be financially worthwhile.

9.2.2   Additional personal allowance

This is a very important relief and should be claimed as a matter of course. It may be claimed by a person not entitled to the married allowance and is intended to help individuals who do not have a husband or wife to assist with bringing up a child or children. Where there is only one child the allowance can be apportioned between the parents as they agree or, failing agreement, in proportion to the length of time that the child resides with each of them during the year. Where there is more than one child it should be possible for each parent to claim one allowance.

In the year of separation the husband receives the married man's allowance and therefore is not entitled to receive the additional personal allowance as well; however, the wife should be able to claim the additional personal allowance in that year.

9.2.3   Mortgage interest relief

The basic conditions for claiming mortgage interest relief are set out in 1.4.2.

If the matrimonial home is transferred to the wife but the husband continues to pay the mortgage interest the husband may be at a disadvantage if he is trying to purchase his own property as well. Where this point is relevant responsibility for the repayment of the mortgage could be transferred to the wife along with the matrimonial home and then the husband could increase his mainten-ance payments to the wife to enable her to make the mortgage repayments. As a result, the husband will enjoy full relief from the maintenance payments (see 9.2.4) and the wife will obtain relief on the mortgage interest payments, at least up to the £30,000 limit. Also, where the husband wishes to purchase a house for himself he will be able to obtain tax relief on interest paid in respect of loans up to £30,000 in his own right.

The position can be more complicated where the hus-band wishes to remain in the matrimonial home. He might decide to raise a second mortgage on the house in order to provide the funds necessary to pay off his wife. The initial reaction might be that loan interest relief would be available as the husband was acquiring his wife's interest in the house but this need not always be so.

A wife's claim to an interest in the matrimonial home could arise in one of several ways. For instance, the matrimonial home might have been conveyed to the husband and wife expressly to hold as beneficial tenants in common in equal shares; or the wife's interest might be by way of a resulting trust, she having provided the whole or part of the purchase price. In the latter case, the most convenient course for the wife would be for her to seek a declaration as to her beneficial interest under Section 17 of the Married Women's Property Act 1882. Again, the wife might have become entitled to her interest in the property as a result of an order in the matrimonial proceedings, for instance a property transfer order under Section 24 of the Matrimonial Causes Act 1973. What must be borne in mind is that relief for mortgage interest will be obtainable only if what the husband is purchasing is his wife's property right. A mere hope or expectation that the court will make an order under Section 24 above is not such a property right and in any case mortgage interest relief will not be due if the husband is simply ordered to pay his wife a capital sum which he raises by remortgaging his house.

In practice the Revenue allows relief for interest paid by the party who continues to live in the former matrimonial home even though he or she does not own an estate or interest in it.

9.2.4 Maintenance payments

In order for maintenance payments to qualify for tax relief they must be made under a legally binding agreement, e.g. a separation agreement or a court order. A separation agreement should record the decision to live apart, specify a regular maintenance payment, set out the arrangements for the children and acknowledge that the agreement is intended on both sides to be legally binding. (A letter signed by both parties may merely indicate an arrangement which does not by itself create legal obligations, so care is required.)

Where a court order is desired, early application should be made to the courts. This takes advantage of a Revenue concession whereby payments under a court order to a spouse and to the children may be backdated for tax purposes to the *date of application*. Even where a later variation of the agreement results in a reclassification of the income for years earlier than the date of application to the courts this cannot result in any change in the way that those payments have been previously treated for tax purposes. Both parties must agree and there must be no undue delay in making the application. The husband will then get full tax relief for the payments made. The payments made will become the income of the recipient for tax purposes. Generally, voluntary payments do not qualify for tax relief to the payer and are not treated as taxable income in the hands of the recipient. Their only relevance may be to determine whether the husband is substantially maintaining the ex-wife for the purposes of claiming the higher personal allowance.

Court orders for maintenance generally take into account the income and tax liabilities of both parties. Tax is deductible from the payment, except where the order directs that they should be paid free of tax, in which case the payments have to be grossed up for all tax purposes.

When drawing up the provisions of any divorce settlement or separation agreement it is essential to ensure that the arrangements are not affected by the anti-avoidance provisions relating to settlements contained in the Taxes Acts. As far as payments to the ex-wife are concerned, payments under a court order or separation agreement should qualify for full tax relief; where under an oral agreement the arrangements are intended to be legally binding the payments may also qualify for tax relief. However, if the husband merely pays directly the expenses of, say, the matrimonial home occupied by the wife, they will not qualify for tax relief.

EXAMPLE 8

After many years of marriage David and Anne decided to separate permanently on 31 March 1985. They have two children, both being privately educated, who need to be provided for under the financial arrangements.

David has agreed to pay Anne £10,000 per annum under a maintenance agreement. He will actually pay her £7,300 net with an effective basic rate deduction of £2,700. For the 1987/88 tax year the position that now applies is compared with the position had there been no separation.

	David £	Anne £	David and Anne £
David's earnings	45,000		45,000
Anne's earnings		2,500	2,500
Investment income	6,000		6,000
	51,000	2,500	53,500
Maintenance paid/received	(10,000)	10,000	
	41,000	12,500	
Less Allowances married			3,795
single	2,425	2,425	2,425
			6,220
Taxable income	£38,575	£10,075	£47,280

Tax thereon	14,934	2,720	20,026
Add Tax retained by David on maintenance	2,700		
Less Tax withheld from Anne on maintenance		(2,700)	
Final liability	£17,634	£20	£20,026

Tax saving following separation:

Tax due			
before separation			20,026
after separation			
David	17,634		
Anne	20		
			17,654
			£2,372

Anne's liability is in fact the tax due on her earnings less her personal allowance, i.e. £2,500 − £2,425 @ 27% = £20·25. It is likely that this will be dealt with under PAYE if the earnings are from an employment.

EXAMPLE 9

The way that court orders for the children are structured is very important if the maximum tax advantage is to be obtained. Court order A directs payment to Anne of £10,000 for herself and £3,500 for each of the two children. Court order B directs a payment to Anne of £10,000 and to each child of £3,500, the net amounts being paid direct to the school bursar:

	Order A	Order B	
	Anne £	Anne £	Each child £
Maintenance payments:			
Anne	10,000	10,000	
Children	7,000		3,500
	17,000		
Other income	5,000	5,000	
Total	22,000	15,000	3,500
Less Allowances	2,425	2,425	2,425
Chargeable	£19,575	£12,575	£1,075
Tax thereon	5,503	3,395	290
Less Basic rate tax on maintenance	(4,590)	(2,700)	(945)
Total liability/ (refund)	£913	£695	(£655)
Net income:			
Net maintenance	12,410	7,300	2,555
Add tax (due)/ overpaid	(913)	(695)	655
		6,605	3,210
		6,420	× 2
	£11,497	£13,025	
Additional net income following court order *B*	£1,528		

Most of the problems are encountered where maintenance payments are made to the children or school fees are paid on their behalf. Tax relief will be obtained on maintenance payments only if:

(a) they are made under a separation agreement or a court order, in favour of the wife for the maintenance of the child (but the payments will then be treated as the wife's income); *or*

(b) they are made under a court order only direct to the child (when the payments will be treated as the child's income thus enabling the child's personal allowances and basic rate band to be utilized).

9.2.5 School fees

Where the father is contractually liable to the school for the payment of fees there can be no advantage for tax purposes, i.e. the payments made will not be allowable in the hands of the father and will not be the child's income.

However, the Revenue does allow relief where the father makes payments direct to the school. This arrangement would normally only be adopted where the mother, who would otherwise receive the maintenance payments under the order as the child's guardian, is considered to be totally irresponsible regarding money, for example because she had an alcohol or similar problem. The procedure would be as follows:

(a) The child enters into a contract with the school under which the latter agrees to educate the child for payment.

(b) The person receiving the school fees (headteacher, bursar or school secretary) must agree to act as agent for the child.

(c) The school fees will be payable in full out of the net amount due under the maintenance order after tax at the basic rate has been deducted from the total amount payable, including the school fees.

It is also possible to avoid varying the maintenance order when the school fees increase by introducing a form of words so as to allow for automatic adjustment.

9.2.6 Small maintenance payments

Small maintenance payments are payments due weekly or monthly under a UK *court order* (maintenance due under any *agreement* is never a small maintenance payment), for the benefit of a separated or divorced spouse, or of a child under 21, within the following limits which were effective from 6 April 1986:

	Weekly £	Monthly £
For the maintenance of a wife or former wife	48	208
To any person for the maintenance, etc. of each child under 21 years	25	108

	Weekly £	Monthly £
Direct to each child under 21 for his own maintenance, etc.	48	208

Small maintenance payments must be paid gross by the husband to the wife or children. Basic and higher rate relief, if claimable, will be given to the husband by permitting him to deduct from his total income for tax purposes payments which fall due in the relevant year of assessment, provided the payments are actually made. Conversely, these payments will be treated as untaxed income of the recipient assessable for the year in which they fall due. Small maintenance payments will often be covered by the recipient's personal allowances so that there will be no additional tax to pay.

9.3 CAPITAL GAINS TAX

As for income tax, the crucial year is the year in which the parties permanently separate and not the year of divorce. In the year of separation the wife's gains up to the date of separation are assessed on the husband (subject to any election for separate assessment, see 2.6.2). After the separation the wife will be assessed on the gains arising to her. Therefore, in the year of separation the husband will be entitled to the annual exemption (£6,600 for 1987/88) and the wife will also be entitled to a separate annual exemption in respect of gains made by her after the date of separation. In the following years each spouse will be separately assessed and each will be entitled to the full annual exemption.

In the year of separation only, assets transferred between the spouses are effected on a no-gain/no-loss basis and the recipient spouse takes over the transferor's base cost and acquisition date under the general rule applying to married persons. Therefore, if the recipient spouse is happy to take over the accrued gains of the donor spouse on this basis, transfers of chargeable assets should take place in the year of separation. This approach applies *throughout* the tax year in which the separation takes place and not just for the period prior to the date of separation.

After the year of separation the rules above can no longer apply. However, for capital gains tax purposes the parties are still considered to be connected persons and it was held in a recent tax case that any transfer of chargeable assets after the year of separation, and before the formal divorce or the issue of the decree absolute, takes place at market value. This can introduce some difficulty. The question arises as to whether the holdover relief described in 1.5.6 can be claimed. It appears that the Revenue takes the view that holdover relief is not available as the transfers between the spouses are not gratuitous but are as a result of an arm's length bargain which would specifically preclude the relief from being applicable. Nevertheless, there is a school of thought which says that holdover relief should apply and where there is no other option, e.g. on the transfer of private company shares, a claim for the relief should be submitted and the point argued. However, in general the advice must be that because of the practical difficulties of arguing against the Inland Revenue's interpretation it must be better to ensure that any transfers of chargeable assets are made during the year of separation if this is at all possible.

Where a married couple separate or are divorced and the husband leaves the matrimonial home but the wife and children continue to occupy it, the principal private residence exemption normally available will continue to apply on the subsequent disposal of the property to the wife after more than two years. As mentioned in 1.5.5 the last 24 months of ownership of any property which has been an individual's principal private residence are exempt in any case. However, the extension of the exemption for more than two years will be lost where the husband purchases another property for himself in the meantime and this then becomes his main residence.

Where the husband transfers part of his interest in the matrimonial home to his spouse and the wife and children continue to live in it then on the eventual sale of the property the husband will be liable to capital gains tax on his share of the gain less his period of occupation in the last 24 months. The wife's share of the gain should be exempt as it arises on her principal private residence.

9.4 INHERITANCE TAX

The critical date for inheritance tax purposes is the date on which the parties divorce, i.e. the date of the decree absolute. Therefore, transfers between spouses prior to that date will normally be exempt; furthermore, the transfers pursuant to a court order which take place after the divorce will also be exempt, provided that they are not intended to confer any gratuitous benefit. All maintenance payments for children and the ex-wife will normally be exempt in any case. However, inheritance tax could possibly be significant where the husband makes substantial transfers of property to the children which are in excess of reasonable maintenance for them and he subsequently dies within seven years of the gift being made.

9.5 STAMP DUTY

For instruments executed after 25 March 1985 *ad valorem* duty is not chargeable on any transfer of property between two parties to a marriage if the instrument is made to implement a court order made on or subsequent to the granting of a divorce, judicial separation or decree of nullity. The exemption is also available where a transfer is made to implement an agreement in contemplation of or in connection with divorce, judicial separation or annulment. Such documents will be liable only to stamp duty of 50p.

9.6 WILLS

Following recent changes in the law any bequest to a former spouse under a will is automatically revoked on divorce. However, if one spouse dies after the date of separation but prior to the decree absolute any bequests in his will to the former spouse will still stand. Therefore it is very important for both parties to execute a new will as soon as possible after the permanent separation.

10 Tax-Efficient Investments

10.1 INVESTMENT STRATEGY

There can never be any easy answers when one is considering investment strategy. This will always be governed by the personal aims and requirements, tastes and priorities of the particular individual concerned. In particular, it is necessary to know what an individual's short-, medium- and long-term income and capital requirements are likely to be and the level of risk that they are prepared to take in order to maximize their return.

It is necessary not only to plan for the future known requirements of the individual, such as to provide funds to pay school fees or for when children get married, but also to cover emergencies such as long-term illness, unemployment, divorce or death.

As has often been said, the tax tail should never be allowed to wag the investment and commercial dog. There is little point in taking advantage of every type of tax relief or shelter available if it means that so much capital is tied up that the individual becomes fully exposed in an emergency.

A prudent approach may be to apportion available funds in the following way:

Emergency fund. The first tranche of capital should be placed in a fund from which it can be drawn immediately and which offers complete security, perhaps a high-interest-yielding building society account.

Low risk/high income/high accessibility fund. A proportion of capital should be placed in low risk investments that can be realized fairly easily at short notice. The aim should be to secure a higher guaranteed net investment return, comprising a mix of income and capital gains, compared to that obtained by the emergency fund. A short-dated gilt-edged security may be appropriate.

High risk/low income/high gains/low accessibility. The third portion of capital could be invested in the higher risk and reward types of investments which would aim to provide a higher net return than the other two funds.

10.2 SHELTERING INCOME

There are a number of ways in which income can be sheltered from a tax liability. This can be achieved by:

(a) Investing in assets that specifically yield a tax-free income, perhaps after a period of time:

- National Savings: yearly plan; ordinary account (first £70); certificates; index-linked third issue; premium bonds.

(b) Making investments, the cost of which is partly or wholly deductible in arriving at an individual's tax liability for the year:

- pension contributions;
- business expansion schemes;
- oil and gas partnerships;
- enterprise zones;
- farming;
- woodlands;
- furnished holiday lettings.

(c) Investing in ways such that the ultimate tax liability arising on income can be deferred either for a specific period or indefinitely, perhaps in expectation of retirement or non-residence:

- offshore money market funds;
- offshore roll-up funds;
- single premium bonds;
- Lloyd's underwriting.

(d) Gifting assets or cash so that any inherent or future income or gains that accrue go to a member of the family who is unable to utilize personal allowances or exemptions that might otherwise be lost:

- deeds of covenant: adult children; grandchildren;
- single premium bonds for minor children;
- bare trustee settlements.

It is obvious that everyone will have different requirements, both personally and financially, and it is therefore essential that all aspects of an individual's personal and financial position and of his investment and gifting philosophy be fully appraised before any fundamental decisions are taken. It will be necessary to consider capital and net spendable income positions both under the current situation and projected over the next few years so that the consequences of taking any particular course of action can be appreciated.

Even where an investment programme is followed, it will still be necessary from time to time to review investments made so that any adjustments considered necessary can be undertaken.

10.3   IDENTIFYING SITUATIONS WHERE ACTION MAY BE NECESSARY

Signs that some personal financial planning is needed may be obtained from the appearance of one or more of the following pointers:

(a) high rates of personal taxation;
(b) substantial unearned income received from sources such as building societies and banks;
(c) tax repayments cannot be obtained because tax credits available are of the non-refundable type;
(d) credit balances on directors' or partners' current accounts in private companies and partnerships where the firms concerned have substantial cash balances at the bank;

(e)   no life assurance premiums paid;
(f)   no pension scheme contributions or retirement annu-
      ity premiums paid;
(g)   taxable income just exceeds the maximum for age
      allowance purposes.

It must be emphasized that the above are merely a
few indicators; each individual's circumstances are quite
different. It is essential that the individual obtains skilled
specialist advice on his chosen investment scheme and
that this advice is properly and effectively co-ordinated by
his professional advisers working in concert.

10.4   PRINCIPAL PRIVATE RESIDENCE

Everyone should consider investing in property not only
for the tax benefits that may follow but for the security
that such investment can offer. It is true that one's
principal private residence probably represents the greatest
investment that most individuals are likely to make and it
is specifically encouraged by the Government. Apart from
the security aspect mentioned above the value of property
in the medium to long term should appreciate at least in
line with inflation.

   The most important considerations are loan interest
relief described at 1.4.2 and the exemption from capital
gains tax, provided certain conditions are met, described
at 1.5.5.

There is no specific relief from a charge to inheritance tax. However, relief will be forthcoming where, for instance, the principal private residence is transferred to the surviving spouse on death.

10.5 CHARITABLE GIVING

A covenant in favour of a charity is a more effective way of giving assistance than paying a lump sum. This is because charities are generally exempt from corporation tax, income tax and capital gains tax provided that the income and gains are applied only for charitable purposes. The benefit arises because the payer is required to deduct income tax at the basic rate from the payments made and the charity is able to recover these deductions as tax repayments.

A covenant in favour of a charity must be capable of running for a minimum of three years or until the death of the covenantor if this is earlier. From 6 April 1986 there is no limit to the amount of covenanted payments made by an individual to a charity that can be deducted in calculating that individual's total income in determining any liability to higher rate tax (see 1.4.3). Relief for higher rates of tax for covenanted payments up to £3,000 was introduced in 1980 and this was increased to £5,000 in 1983 and to £10,000 in 1985. As stated above, the charity is able to recover from the Revenue the whole of the *basic rate tax* deducted at source by the payer.

There is a measure of inflexibility in this approach in that where a deed of covenant is executed in favour of a particular charity those payments must continue to be paid to that charity during the life of the deed. However, there are alternatives. An individual may execute a deed of covenant in favour of an agency charity (such as the Charities Aid Foundation) which will receive the money for the benefit of charitable purposes. The money remains in a separate fund accruing income as time goes by and a convenantor is able to direct how the money is to be used to make specific gifts to charities as and when it is appropriate to do so; to facilitate this he can be provided with a special cheque-book so that he can make the payments in person direct to the chosen charity. A further alternative may be for the individual to create his own charitable settlement and to make payments to it by way of deed of covenant.

Where an individual wishes to benefit a charity with a single donation, tax benefits can still be obtained by executing a deposited covenant. Under this arrangement an interest free loan is made to the charity out of which the net covenanted payments due during the life of the deed are taken; as these net payments are taken up the charity can claim the corresponding income tax repayments. In this way the charity benefits further as it can invest the moneys borrowed and receive the income therefrom totally free of tax.

The use of a personal charitable settlement is likely to appeal to wealthy individuals who wish to set funds aside for charitable purposes but where they may not wish to be tied to any particular charity.

Gifts into a settlement of this type are exempt from capital gains tax, inheritance tax and stamp duty. Continued funding of the settlement can be dealt with by way of a deed of covenant in favour of the trustees. Except for trading income all income received by the settlement will be exempt from tax and any tax deducted at source can be recovered from the Inland Revenue. Consequently, this can be a very effective way for a higher rate taxpayer to create his own gross fund which he can use to benefit charitable causes with both capital and income.

A new arrangement was brought into operation on 6 April 1987 which permits an employer to arrange with his employees that he will deduct a regular amount from their weekly or monthly pay and pass it over to an agency which will deal with its disbursement to various charities nominated by the employees. Such payments will rank as tax deductible to the contributing employees and tax relief will be given automatically through the employer's payroll. The amount to be deducted and paid over in this way is to be limited to £120 a year for each employee.

APPENDIX A. INCOME TAX RATES AND ALLOWANCES 1987/88

Rates of income tax

Rate %	Band of taxable income £	Cumulative tax £
27	0–17,900	4,833
40	17,901–20,400	5,833
45	20,401–25,400	8,083
50	25,401–33,300	12,033
55	33,301–41,200	16,378
60	over 41,200	—

Personal allowances

	£
Single person's allowance	2,425
Wife's earned income allowance (maximum)	2,425
Married man's allowance	3,795
Dependent relative – male claimant	100
– 'single' female claimant	145
Daughter's or son's services	55
Blind person's relief	540
Additional personal allowance ('single-parent' families)	1,370
Widow's bereavement allowance	1,370

Single person's age allowance		
65–80:	2,960	Income
over 80:	3,070	limit
Married man's age allowance		£9,800
65–80:	4,675	
over 80:	4,845	
Life assurance premiums paid on policies in force on 13 March 1984	15% deduction from total premiums paid	

Note

Detailed rules as to the entitlement to any of these allowances will need to be checked in individual cases.

APPENDIX B.   CAPITAL TAXES 1987/88

Inheritance tax (effective from 17 March 1987)

Lower limit £	Upper limit £	Rate of Tax £	Tax to top of band £
nil	90,000	nil	nil
90,000	140,000	30	15,000
140,000	220,000	40	47,000
220,000	330,000	50	102,000
330,000	—	60	—

These rates also apply to lifetime transfers made within the three-year period prior to the date of death.

For lifetime transfers made more than three years but less than seven years before death, only a proportion of the full charge is applicable, as follows:

Years between transfers and death	Proportion of full charge %
3–4	80
4–5	60
5–6	40
6–7	20

Capital gains tax (effective from 6 April 1987)

Annual exemptions
   individuals   £6,600
   trusts   £3,300
Rate of tax   30%

APPENDIX C. NATIONAL INSURANCE CONTRIBUTIONS 1987/88

Class 1 Employed	*Employees*	*Employers*
Not contracted out –		
on all earnings		
up to £38·99 per week	*nil*	*nil*
up to £64·99 per week	5·00%	5·00%
up to £99·99 per week	7·00%	7·00%
up to £149·99 per week	9·00%	9·00%
up to £295 per week	9·00%	10·45%
on excess over £295 per week	*nil*	10·45%
Contracted out – *on all earnings*		
up to £38·99 per week	*nil*	*nil*
up to £64·99 per week		
on first £39	5·00%	5·00%
on balance	2·85%	0·90%
up to £99·99 per week		
on first £39	7·00%	7·00%
on balance	4·85%	2·90%
up to £149·99 per week		
on first £39	9·00%	9·00%
on balance	6·85%	4·90%
up to £295 per week		
on first £39	9·00%	10·45%
on balance	6·85%	6·35%
on excess over £295 per week	*nil*	10·45%

Classes 2 and 4 Self-employed

Class 2 fixed per week   £3·85
   no liability if earning below £2,125 per year
Class 4 earnings related   6·3%*
   on profits between £4,590 and £15,340 a year

Class 3 Non-employed

Voluntary rate per week   £3·75

* Half these contributions rank for income tax relief.

APPENDIX D.   CARS AND CAR PETROL 1987/88

| | Cars | | |
	Under 4 years old £	4 years old or more £	Car petrol £
A. Cars with original market value less than £19,250 and having a cylinder capacity:			
1400cc or less	525	350	480
1400cc to 2000cc	700	470	600
over 2000cc	1,100	725	900
B. Cars with original market value less than £19,250 and not having a cylinder capacity:			
less than £6,000	525	350	480
£6,000 to £8,499	700	470	600
£8,500 to £19,249	1,100	725	900
C. Cars with original market value of £19,250 or more:			
£19,250 to £29,000	1,450	970	900
over £29,000	2,300	1,530	900

Notes

(a) Where there is preponderant business use (defined as more than 18,000 miles a year), both the car and car petrol benefits are reduced by half.

(b) Where the car is not available for a period of time

(normally at least 30 consecutive days in a year), both the car and car petrol benefits are reduced proportionately.

(c) Where the car has only insubstantial business use (defined as less than 2,500 miles a year) or it is an additional car provided by the employer, the car benefit is increased by a half. There is no increase in the car petrol benefit.

(d) The car petrol benefits apply only to cars made available by the employer; the normal benefit-in-kind legislation applies where petrol is provided by an employer for an individual's own car, hire car, etc.